SHERMAN PARK

SHERMAN PARK

A LEGACY *of* DIVERSITY IN MILWAUKEE

PAUL H. GEENEN

THE History PRESS

Published by The History Press
Charleston, SC 29403
www.historypress.net

First published 2012

Manufactured in the United States

ISBN 978.1.60949.641.8

Library of Congress CIP data applied for.

Notice: The information in this book is true and complete to the best of our knowledge. It is offered without guarantee on the part of the author or The History Press. The author and The History Press disclaim all liability in connection with the use of this book.

To our grandchildren: Mikaal, Shanti, Jordan, Cassidy, Narain, Sanju, Felix and Theron.

CONTENTS

ACKNOWLEDGEMENTS

The author wishes to thank those who shared their memories about life in Sherman Park and made their photos available: Mayor Tom Barrett, Brian Beaudet, Alan Borsuk, Patrick Curley, Fred Curzn, Bill Drew, Colleen Fitzgerald, Patricia Geenen, Sarah Geenen, Michael Geenen, William Geenen, Kathy Geiger, Michele Goldstein, James Gramling, Bradley Hausler, Paul Henningsen, Martin Hintz, Steven Hintz, Carolyn Jackson, Jeff Jackson, Julie Jackson, Marilyn Johannsen, Howard Karsh, Larry LeBlanc, Mordecai Lee, Dester Martin, Paul Mathews, Chris McAuliffe, Byron and Judy McBride, Jonathan McBride, Mikle McBride, Chris McCreary, Jeff McCreary, Mary McCreary, Kathy and Frank Mulvey, Michael Mulvey, Patrick Mulvey, Rolfe and Mary Nervig, Ruth Nervig, John Norquist, Karl Pearson-Cater, Kay and Otto Pena, Kristin Powers, Bill Rumpf, Ryan and Joan Sattler, Bill Sell, Arlene Skwierawski, Nancy Spransey, Elaine Stalheim, Cecil Sutphen, David Sutphen, Mona Sutphen, Anita Thompson, Cory Thompson, Edward and Theresa Valent, Magnolia Verser, Tieg Whaely-Smith and others.

INTRODUCTION

The idea for this book came from a dinner with my wife, Patricia Geenen; Jonathan McBride, a member of the White House staff; and myself at the Old Ebbitt Grill, a place that fairly reeks of power and prestige, located several blocks from the White House in Washington, D.C. My wife and I had been Jonathan's lunch guests at the White House Dining Room, where we had admired the photos of President Obama's recent activities, caught a glimpse of Vice President Joe Biden leaving the premises and dined near the Situation Room.

My wife and I were bubbling over with excitement from our experiences of the day. This was a far cry from our days of raising a family in a near west side Milwaukee neighborhood called Sherman Park, where we struggled to get the attention of our local alderman and other city officials. We decided the story of Sherman Park needed to be told. It was important to get the history of this Milwaukee neighborhood from 1960 to 1990 and residents' stories documented.

A University of Wisconsin–Milwaukee (UWM) class oral history project was completed in 1996 as part of Sherman Park Community Association's twenty-fifth anniversary celebration. UWM students had interviewed over fifty members, preserving important recollections about their struggles and challenges of the times. To this excellent resource, I added interviews of over sixty people of three generations who lived in Sherman Park.

This has been a difficult book to write. Our family lived in Sherman Park for thirty years, moving to the area in 1976. This neighborhood was a large part of our identity, and when we moved to a larger house on the Eastside of Milwaukee, we continued to tell people for a long time that we "used to live in Sherman Park."

Many of our closest friends come from this community. The neighborhood called Sherman Park is sizable, and at every interview, people made additional recommendations of people I should talk to. It was impossible to reach everyone given my deadline.

Founding members were members of the '60s generation. They thought they could do anything. They could fight the political structure and could single-handedly integrate the entire Milwaukee Public Schools, and they believed that love was enough to cure physically damaged adopted children. The lessons learned, the successes and the disappointments, make for a complicated story.

The experiment did not end with the first generation of Sherman Park members. Their children learned valuable lessons about how to be successful in a diverse world. They learned how to deal with physical danger, relate to diverse cultures and advocate for change. We get more insights into this in the interviews of the next generation.

And last, and most important of all, the grandchildren are the crown jewels of this experiment. These kids are completely comfortable in multiple cultural environments and carry on the founding principles of Sherman Park in new ways never envisioned fifty years ago.

CHAPTER 1
TENSION!

1960 to 1970

A Segregated Country

The 1960s were a time of social unrest and change in our country. In 1963, President John F. Kennedy was shot, and Dr. Martin Luther King led the March on Washington that same year. On the National Mall, at one of our country's largest political gatherings, several hundred thousand blacks and whites heard King's "I Have A Dream" speech. In 1964, Congress approved the Gulf of Tonkin Resolution, starting the divisive, eight-year Vietnam War. In 1968, both Dr. Martin Luther King and Robert F. Kennedy were assassinated.

African Americans were being driven out of the south by what many of them describe as "the hangings." They migrated north, attracted by jobs where they could earn four times what they had been earning in the cotton fields. Following the rail lines north, some found Chicago a city too large, and it jarred with their rural roots. They continued north to the more manageable city of Milwaukee. Rachael Adams was one of those migrants. She said in a 1996 interview that she moved to Milwaukee during the civil rights movement because "they were having sit-ins and battles with whites against blacks and blacks against whites, killing people and shooting people."

Between 1960 and 1967, almost thirty thousand African Americans moved to Milwaukee, adding 50 percent more people to the population in an area bounded by the Milwaukee River and Twenty-seventh Street to the east and west and Capital Drive and State Street to the north and south. New migrants from the south were crowded into homes that were plagued with vermin, uncertain plumbing and heating and unrepaired windows. Milwaukee's central city had a high concentration of children, with 43 percent of the African American population being under fifteen years old, compared to the city as a whole with 28 percent. The core was surrounded by better homes on wide, tree-lined streets similar to "many poorer white neighborhoods in the city," as Aukofer mentions in his book *City with A Chance*.

The 1966 Model Cities Program replaced substandard housing located just south of Walnut Street in the central city with the Hillside Housing Complex. This created a ripple effect. African Americans who had been working in the tanneries, meatpacking plants and foundries started buying, using their accumulated savings, the attractive and affordable homes in the Fifth Ward, a neighborhood with a small park in its midst, called Sherman Park. This neighborhood, that would take its name from that park, with its mix of renters and homeowners, blacks and whites, running the entire gamut of educational backgrounds, would be studied and written about for the next thirty years by researchers and authors trying to understand the key elements of its success that could be duplicated in other neighborhoods across our country.

The political leadership of the city was insensitive to the plight of the African American community. The clearance of land for the freeway system that started in 1963 destroyed the community's Bronzeville neighborhood. The Milwaukee Public School Board kept black students in segregated, inferior, classrooms. Jobs were plentiful in the dirty, hot, odiferous and dangerous tanneries, meatpacking plants and foundries, but unions were keeping blacks out of the trades. African Americans were underrepresented in the city's police and fire departments.

In the early 1960s, overt racial prejudice was socially acceptable, even by public officials. For example, in 1962, Fred Lins—the chairman of Milwaukee's Social Development Commission, an agency charged with funneling federal dollars to those who were the most needy—was quoted in the *Milwaukee Journal* as saying, "The Negroes look so much alike that you can't identify the ones that committed the crime." According to Aukofer, Lins was also quoted describing African Americans as being "an awful mess of them have(ing) an IQ of nothing." In the same year, eighteen of Milwaukee's nineteen aldermen voted down four times an open housing ordinance proposed by Vel Phillips, Milwaukee's first African American city council member.

On July 25, 1963, thirty-four African American members of the Committee on a Statement of Concern published a letter in both the *Milwaukee Journal* and the *Sentinel* asking Mayor Henry Maier to take a leadership role on the city's racial problems. In August of the same year, nine members of Congress of Racial Equality (CORE) staged a sit-in at Milwaukee County Court House requesting that Lins be fired. In 1964, Governor George Wallace was supported by over 31 percent of Wisconsin voters in his bid for president and his support of abolishing the Civil Rights Act, which called for equal public accommodations and employment opportunities for all, according to Aukofer.

Milwaukee at this time was a "hyper segregated city," as Squires and Valent state in *Sherman Park*. Lending institutions, appraisers and insurance and real estate companies, using a practice called "red lining," worked together to keep African Americans in their segregated housing. Whites were moving to the suburbs to snap up newly built homes using Federal Housing Administration (FHA) and Veterans Affairs (VA) mortgages. Such choices were not available for African Americans, though. According to Juliet Saltman's book *A Fragile Movement*, in 1967 there were only sixty-six African Americans living in the ring of twenty-five suburban communities that surrounded Milwaukee. An FHA study that same year documented the fact that only 320 African Americans out of 90,000 African Americans residing in Milwaukee were living between Twenty-seventh Street and Sherman Boulevard.

Milwaukee's Race Riots

African Americans moved from writing letters to protesting against the unresponsiveness of the political structure. Early in 1966, the NAACP Youth Council picketed the Eagles Club located on the 2400 block of Wisconsin Avenue, protesting the club's white-only membership policy. The Milwaukee Aerie of the Eagles Club, with its 5,400 members, was the second largest Eagles Club in the entire country and had national significance, as well as seventeen judges, ten county supervisors, ten aldermen and a member of the city election commission on its membership rolls. Milwaukee's mayor, Henry Maier, was a member and the state's governor, Warren Knowles, was an honorary member. The rationale for membership in this "whites-only" club was that one's private life had nothing to do with one's public life. The NAACP Youth Council protests moved next to Judge Cannon's home, where they created a carnival atmosphere complete with an old, hand-painted truck selling popcorn and candy bars. White youths threw eggs, bottles and fireworks at the protestors. After several nights of four and five hundred people camped outside the judge's home, National Guardsmen were called in to surround his house. The NAACP youths moved to several other judges' homes to continue their protests, and on August 10, 1966, the NAACP office in Milwaukee was destroyed with a bomb.

The anger and frustration from living in crowded substandard housing and lack of access to better paying jobs caused the African American community to explode. The Milwaukee Police Department's attempts to control an altercation at a tavern near Third and Center Streets quickly grew into widespread violence on Sunday, July 30, 1967. Governor Warren Knowles called out 2,300 National Guard troops, and Mayor Maier imposed a ten-day curfew covering the area from the Milwaukee River to Fifty-first Street and from State Street to Capital Drive. Patrick Curley, who grew up near Center and Forty-sixth Streets, remembers seeing a number of police ambulances emptying out a gun shop located near his home on Center. The police loaded every gun in the shop into their trucks and took the load to their staging area. Jack Koplin, who was inventory control manager at Gimbels Third Street store at the time, remembers seeing waist-high stacks of ammunition stored in the parking garage adjacent to the store on the Monday after the riot.

People were acting unpredictably with the disintegration of order. Police Chief Harold Brier ordered that anyone caught on the street after midnight would be arrested. Officer Felmers Chaney, one of Milwaukee's first African American police officers, followed those orders and arrested a white *Milwaukee Journal* reporter who was still on the street at 5:00 a.m. Many of the stores on Third Avenue were destroyed, but Virginia McKinney's store, Diane's Uniforms, located right across from Gimbels, was not touched, perhaps because she was well known in the African American community. Warren Braun, a Milwaukee alderman, remembers seeing a line of National Guard trucks driving down the freeway.

Curley tells the story of a woman on his block whose husband was a police officer. The woman was recording the license numbers of African Americans driving on Forty-sixth Street just in case there was any trouble. The riots in July 1967 left 3 dead, 100 injured and 1,740 people arrested, and they lasted for five hours. The riots and the ensuing curfew that extended to Fifty-first

Street, miles from the original site of the disturbance, set an "eerie tone," Curley recalls.

The Open Housing Marches

Directly west of the most densely populated African American neighborhood was the neighborhood that came to be called Sherman Park in the early 1970s, an area defined by the existing Fifth Ward, Thirty-fifth to Sixtieth, North to Keefe. In the 1960s, the churches and synagogues lent their names to their adjoining neighborhoods. For example, the neighborhood around St. Catherine's, at Fifty-first and Center, was called "St. Kate's."

Most of the homes here had been built from the 1920s through the 1940s for professional and working-class European immigrants. The duplex and single-family houses built east and west of Sherman Boulevard mostly had smaller yards, while many of the homes on Grant, Sherman and Fifty-first Boulevards were built of brick and stone with larger yards and double rows of elm trees on the boulevards. This mix of duplexes and single-family homes stimulated economic diversity.

The Catholic, Protestant and Jewish congregations attracted young families who saw this as a great neighborhood to raise children in. Grant Boulevard was called "clergy row," and in addition to those of the cloth, teachers, nurses and social workers lived there. St. Catherine's, St. Anne's, St. John's, St. Stephen's and Sherman Park Lutheran each had their own parochial grade schools. People worked for the Milwaukee Road, Masterlock or A.O. Smith, all located nearby. Kids either went to the parochial high school, Messmer, on Capitol Drive, or the public high school, Washington, located on Sherman Boulevard. The alleys were filled with kids playing basketball, tag and other games, and they walked to Sherman Park and Washington Park for sledding and ice skating.

In the mid-'60s, more African Americans were moving into the section between Thirty-fifth and Sherman Boulevard, although the numbers were small. The priests at St. Catherine's were giving sermons encouraging parishioners to get involved in the social concerns of their neighborhood and their city. The Conways had moved to Grant Boulevard ten years before, despite their realtor's attempts to steer them to the Brady Street neighborhood. They began meeting with the Social Concerns Committee of St. Catherine, some of whom lived on Grant Blvd.

In 1965, Marilyn and Walter Johannsen, who had moved onto Fifty-first Street in the late '60s, joined the Social Concerns Committee at St. Catherine's with the Conways. In 1967, after the riots, the open housing marches led by Father James Groppi, who served at St. Boniface Catholic Church, near the intersection of Center and Teutonia Streets, and the anti-war demonstrations prompted the members of St. Catherine's Social Concern Committee to get involved in social action. The Conways, Johannsens, Danforths, Mazureks and Siebolds were bringing food for meal programs at St. Boniface and supporting open housing.

St. Catherine's was a conservative congregation with a large number of people with German heritage who attended church regularly and viewed it as their anchor. It was a somewhat divided congregation, politically, with a traditional service in the main sanctuary and a folk mass in the basement where the Johannsens' son Chris played the guitar. There was considerable disagreement among the four priests who led the parish over the Vietnam War and open housing. The perception of some Catholic critics of the civil rights marches in the south led by Dr. Martin Luther King was that this was a political rather than a moral issue. According to Bill Sell, one of the priests, Archbishop Cousins resisted forces that called on him to control Father Groppi, a vocal and highly visible open housing advocate, saying "Jim Groppi is doing things that I can't do."

Things were starting to change. In 1965, some blocks were experiencing "white flight" when as few as three or four homes on a block were sold to African Americans. The Conways tell the story of an African American couple who toured a Grant Boulevard home next to theirs and offered a cashiers check to the owner to purchase the home on the spot. The owner told the couple that he wanted to think about it and talk to his neighbors. The couple responded by raising their offer twice, by $2,000 each time. The neighbor contacted city hall and was told, according to John, that African Americans were not allowed there and that "we are not moving in that direction yet." The African American couple left in disappointment and never returned.

In August 1967, 250 young men, women and a few children, members of the NAACP Youth Council, led by Father Groppi, marched across the Sixth Street Viaduct for an open housing demonstration in Kosciuszko Park on the near south side, according to Jones in his book *The Selma of the North*. Thirty white police officers, eleven police cars and a paddy wagon protected the marchers as 13,000 angry South Siders screamed epithets and threw garbage at them. The police officers fired shotguns into the air to disperse

A worried Father Groppi is guarded by two NAACP Youth Council members while a policeman in the background maintains separation between the angry crowds (1967). *Courtesy of Milwaukee County Historical Museum.*

the angry crowd. The "dazed" and "bewildered" marchers returned to the NAACP Youth Council's Freedom House on Fifteenth Street. Shortly after their return, the center was firebombed by a passing car, according to Aukofer. Margaret Rozga, Father Groppi's wife, has a different explanation in her book *200 Nights and One Day.* She wrote that police, responding to a report of a sniper, fired tear gas canisters into the house and started the fire. A handwritten sign in the basement of St. Boniface's expressed the hope the community had for open housing, "Black Power + White Power = Community Power," Aukofer reported.

People have clear recollections of the open housing marches. Curley recalls being invited by a friend, Les Seibold, to go down to St. Boniface's. Once there, Seibold said, "Let's walk a while," and they joined the demonstrators. When a nearby house went up in flames, they both hurriedly left. McKinney recalls a customer rushing out of her uniform store on Third Avenue in fear when one of Father Groppi's Fair Housing Marches was passing in front of her store. McKinney went to the customer's home to return the change.

In 1968, the Supreme Court called housing segregation "a relic of slavery" and affirmed open housing in its *Jones v. Mayer* decision. The assassination of Martin Luther King on April 4, 1968, moved Congress to pass the Fair Housing Act. On April 30, 1968, Milwaukee's city council passed an open housing law, even though earlier in the year Mayor Henry Maier thought open housing was "an unworthy cause," according to Aukofer. A year later, a HUD audit showed that African Americans were still being discriminated against in 62 percent of housing sales and 72 percent of rental situations.

The first effort by St. Catherine's Social Concerns Committee to get involved politically was in 1968 when it worked to replace Alderman Mark Ryan with a new elected official who supported open housing. Social Concerns Committee member Peter Mursurick offered to run, but the local Democrats supported a more centrist candidate, Ron Flintrop. Flintrop ran a weak campaign and lost. This experience made people realize that they could not rely on the political structure and that they needed to organize themselves.

Sherman Park

After the 1967 riots, things returned to normal in the neighborhood around St. Catherine's. People were again riding the buses and walking to the Sherman Theater. The Christian Youth Organization soccer team was playing at Washington Park, and Sherman School at Fifty-first and Locust offered the best set of basketball rims in town. On Sunday, after mass, the bakery across from St. Catherine's was packed with people buying sweet rolls and buns for Sunday dinner. An independent five-and-dime between Forty-eight and Forty-ninth Streets was where neighborhood kids bought their candy. Fourth of July parties in Sherman Park continued to be hosted by the Seibolds and the Conways.

Beth Jehudah—an Orthodox synagogue, located on Fifty-second Street, dedicated on December 24, 1950, and led by Rabbi Jacob Twerski—was part of this community. Rabbi Jacob Twerski had started Beth Jehudah around 1939 on the near east side and was famous for his Talmudic scholarship and ability to connect with people, according to Gurda in his book *One People*. In earlier years, Westside residents had welcomed the Jewish community when they had moved into the neighborhood from the central city.

A sizeable Jewish community populated the Sherman Park area in the late 1960s. Jewish shops on Center included the Guten Delicatessen; Berger's Grocery at Forty-ninth and Center; and the Chicago Bakery, also on Forty-ninth. Regina's Cheesecakes, specializing in custom wedding cakes, later replaced Chicago Bakery. Burleigh Street had the Goodman-Bensman Funeral Home and Kohl's grocery store. This grocery store was the launching pad for the Kohl brothers' chain of Kohl's Food Stores and Kohl's department stores. Bubrick's Food Market and Miller's bakery, famous for its rye bread, were also located here. The Beth El Ner Tamid's Conservative synagogue, located in the triangle between Roosevelt, Fond du Lac and Sherman, could seat a thousand members.

In 1967, the area that would soon be called Sherman Park had the city's highest concentration of synagogues in the city, with two Conservative and four Orthodox congregations, according to Gurda in *One People.* But that was changing as their members were moving to the suburbs of Shorewood, Whitefish Bay, Fox Point, Bayside, Glendale, River Hills and Mequon. The Jewish shop owners closed one by one after their kids were raised and left. "As people became more successful, they were drawn to the suburban style [of] living," according to Alan Borsuk. Beth Jehudah stayed, as it had found a permanent home in Sherman Park.

The Freeways

In 1968, the Milwaukee County Expressway Commission started purchasing homes in the block-wide stretch between Meinecke and North Avenue and from Sherman Boulevard to Sixth Street at prices that sometimes did not even cover the mortgages on the property owners' homes. Public hearings were scheduled with short notice so that surrounding owners would not know where the "center line alignment and width" of the freeway would be until it was too late, according to Cutler in *Milwaukee's Growing Pains.* Property values were dropping sharply in the central city where 1,600 homes had been cleared for new freeways. Home values were plummeting on the land surrounding the freeway right of way. Ted Seaver, a neighborhood organizer from the UWM area in Milwaukee, protested against the poor quality housing that was being provided for people who had lost their homes from land cleared for the planned freeways.

By 1969, the Milwaukee County Expressway Commission had acquired the homes on a three-mile right of way, parallel to North Avenue, running from the Hillside Interchange to Sherman Boulevard, for the Park Freeway West. Dester Martin said in a 2006 interview that the construction of the expressway was "as if the blood was taken out of the black community," and he felt like it was "intentional, structured, planned…to neutralize economic development" in the African American community.

Some of the people on the Social Concerns Committee at St. Catherine's started moving their attention to the construction of the Park Freeway West. Wally Johannsen became one of the first members of the committee to oppose the freeways.

The Social Concerns Committee at St. Catherine's organized around the issues of racial steering and the clearing of the freeway land. Its resolve to stay and fight rather than move to the suburbs created a stable island of resolute diversity on Grant and Fifty-first Boulevards. Young families, attracted by the diversity and the value of the houses, were drawn to these middle-class enclaves.

The Muzureks, Conways, Siebolds and Johannsens put the word out to their friends about the features of their neighborhood and recruited new families for the block. Others found Grant and Fifty-first by accident, drawn in by the quality of the homes and the canopy of elm trees that covered the length of the entire block. The Fourth of July parties in Sherman Park, annual block parties and neighbors welcoming new neighbors were continuing traditions of hospitality and community that attracted new home buyers.

St. Catherine's played an important role in developing a core group of politically astute people who would move forward with their own organization to address the forces that were attacking their neighborhood. People like John Conway and Marilyn Johannsen realized that they had to go outside of the structure of St. Catherine's to get the resources they needed to address their community's problems.

The Sherman Park Community Association (SPCA) began forming in 1965, according to John Conway, as part of St. Catherine's Social Concerns Committee. However, the SPCA's ten-year anniversary brochure describes the beginning of SPCA differently: "In the early autumn of 1970 a handful of Westside residents met to form the Sherman Park Community Association." Founding members listed in this 1981 brochure include Rita and John Conway, Betsy and Bob Daniels, Marilyn and Walter Johannsen, Lila and Mike Kelly, Fran and Pete Mazurek, Marci and Jim Mills and Cari and Bob Repasky.

The birth of the Sherman Park Community Association in 1970 was to make the Fifth Ward of Milwaukee's Northwest side a great place to raise families. The new community group consisted of neighbors looking out for each other, and the community itself would become a mecca of diversity where people would be accepted for who they were.

SPCA would establish three standing committees: Housing, Education and the Expressway Committees. The Housing Committee would start by working on absentee-owned homes in poor repair, the Education Committee would address the segregated schools in the neighborhood and the Expressway Committee would fight the construction of the Park West Freeway, which, if built, would divide their neighborhood.

The organization was founded "not in response to an outside threat, but to improve the quality of life in the Fifth Ward of Milwaukee's Northwest side," according to Edward Valent and Gregory Squires in their paper "Sherman Park." Diversity and racial inclusivity were highly valued. SPCA had a budget in 1971 of $1,247, most of which was for the newsletter, which was started in February of the same year. Marilyn Johannsen was editor of the SPCA's newsletter for many years.

The Fifth Ward, which would soon be called Sherman Park, at the close of the '60s had 38,887 residents in the area between North and Keefe, Thirty-fifth to Sixtieth Street, with 202 of them being African American, according to Squires. Jim Gramling describes this as a time when "just the right combination of people (got) together." The commitment, creativity, energy and political savvy of the SPCA would catch a lot of people's attention.

CHAPTER 2

THE URBAN PIONEERS

1970 to 1980

Moving In!

The beautiful homes and the racial diversity of Sherman Park attracted many families. In summer of 1971, two couples, good friends Ryan and Joan Sattler and Tom and Nancy Gonzanna, were driving around the Westside of Milwaukee and found Grant Boulevard. The street had homes of brick, lannon stone or stucco, with leaded glass windows. Most had spacious dining rooms with built-in cabinets and comfortable living rooms complete with hardwood floors and fireplaces. Ryan Sattler called their realtor, although they feared that they could not afford "such a nice house" on his salary as transportation manager at Kohl's Food Stores. A few years back, Ryan and Joan had met at Alverno College, where Joan was an assistant teacher at Alverno College Campus School. Joan had campaigned for Vel Phillips, who became Milwaukee's first African American alderman, and the Sattlers were part of an ecumenical church at Twenty-first and Highland that emphasized social justice issues. They had two young children, three-year-old Peter and one-year-old Paul, and they wanted a house in a neighborhood where their children could be raised in a diverse environment.

Their realtor insisted that the Sattlers look at more homes, but they quickly submitted an offer to purchase the home on Grant. They moved in August 1971. They found most of their neighbors accepting of their views, except for one who turned from being friendly to ceasing to speak to them at all once he became aware of the Sattlers' support of integration. Peter and Fran Mazurek, Marcy and Jim Mill and the Conways, all members of St. Catherine's, warmly welcomed the Sattlers to Sherman Park. Realtors were blanketing homeowners on Grant Boulevard with flyers that said, "We have buyers looking for your home." This practice, called "block busting," was a common real estate practice that was legal at the time. Families not comfortable with integration were moving, and "the block turned (over) entirely within the next couple of years," according to Ryan.

Racially mixed couples were attracted to the diversity of Sherman Park. Sometime around 1972, Cecil and Judy Sutphen, a mixed couple, African American and Jewish, with a blended family of four children, were looking for a home as they had outgrown their apartment at Seventeenth and Atkinson. Their youngest son, David, had just arrived, and their landlord said four children were too many for their apartment. The couple from Kansas City, Missouri, had been married across the border in Topeka, Kansas. When they said their vows, it was a twenty-year felony for an African American to marry a Caucasian in Missouri. Cecil was working for the National Labor Relations board, and they leapt at the chance to move to Milwaukee, where he took a position with the NLRB in Wisconsin.

They had looked for houses on the Eastside of Milwaukee, but one day Judy Sutphen got lost and found a street "with elm trees that formed a canopy for blocks," as she told her husband. It caught their eye. Their offer was accepted on a two-story, dark cream brick home with wide, full-length, double patio-style front windows. The original owner had gone into a nursing home, and the present owner had to sell it for health reasons. The house needed a lot of work, including electrical and plumbing, Cecil recalled.

Families that had adopted across racial lines were also attracted to Sherman Park. The 1967 Supreme Court decision *Loving v. Virginia* that made interracial marriages legal also legalized transracial adoptions. By 1970, there were 2,500 transracial adoptions finalized in the country. But there was resistance to transracial adoption. In 1972, the National Association of Black Social Workers (NABSW) said that "placement of black children in white homes for any reason" was wrong. They called transracial adoption "unnatural, artificial, and unnecessary." Cenie J. Williams, president of the NABSW, argued that temporary foster and even institutional placements were preferred to adoption by white families, according to the Adoption History Project by the Department of History at the University of Oregon.

Cecil and Judy Sutphen's original home at 2424 North Grant Boulevard. This home was placed on the National Register of historic homes on March 23, 1995. *Courtesy of James Baker.*

In 1973, Judy and Byron McBride were living in Merrill, Wisconsin, with their family of two birth daughters and two adopted biracial sons. At the time, Catholics and Protestants did not talk to each other in Merrill, let alone talk to a couple with African American children, Judy remembers. Byron was leaving the Wisconsin Correctional Division, where he worked as a psychologist, to take a job in Milwaukee. The McBrides had read an article in the *Milwaukee Journal* written by Margo Huston about African Americans who had moved to Milwaukee's suburbs. The McBrides telephoned Huston and eventually were connected to Marilynn and Walter Johannsen in the Sherman Park neighborhood.

The McBrides bought a house at Forty-sixth and Townsend despite their realtor's warning that "you don't want to send your kids" to Townsend, the neighborhood school. The neighborhood's middle and elementary schools were totally African American, but the McBrides felt that "we wouldn't want our white girls to pick up the values of any community in which we didn't feel comfortable raising our black kids," according to a quote in the article Huston published about the McBrides in 1973.

The McBrides enrolled their four children at Townsend School. The McBrides' oldest daughter, Rebecca, would soon be going to Peckham Middle School, which was black, while Steuban Middle School was white. Judy immediately joined the Sherman Park Education Committee as she was convinced that this would be a good place to raise their family and that these neighborhood schools could be saved.

In 1974, Huston published a second article about Amy and Rebecca McBride, who at the age of seven and eleven, had founded "The Friendly Club" with half black and half white membership as proof that "we can get along together and that we love each other." Other members of the club were Billi Jo Mason, age eight; Donna Rouse, age nine; and Chris Matter, age ten.

A network of adoptive families began to promote Sherman Park as a place to raise a diverse family. The McBrides spoke enthusiastically about how lucky they were to stumble into the Sherman Park neighborhood. Through their involvement with the Wisconsin Open Door Society, they met other adoptive families who had adopted interracially, and the McBrides felt that they were living with people who were on the same page as they were. Integrated families already living in Sherman Park, including the Yeos and the Perrys, also promoted the neighborhood. In 1975, Tom and Nancy Kruse moved into their new home on Grant Boulevard with their two adopted African American children. Tom Kruse and Bruce Yeo worked together at A.O. Smith, and Tom heard about Sherman Park from Yeo. The Kruses also heard about Sherman Park from Arnie and Eunice Perry while Arnie was a Lutheran pastor at a church in Wauwatosa. The Kruses snapped up a home on Grant Boulevard that became available through an estate.

Nancy remembers: "It was so good not to feel strange because our kids didn't match us." Her strong memories included ice skating and picnics at Sherman Park, the sledding and ice skating at Washington Park, kids riding their big wheels down the block and neighbors watching out for your kids. Her neighbor Mary Ann Harris watched out for her children and would call Nancy if her kids were misbehaving.

Thomas and Carolyn Jackson clipped and saved Huston's articles in the *Milwaukee Journal* about the McBrides. The Jacksons wanted to live in an integrated neighborhood. The family would follow the McBrides and buy a house in Sherman Park in the same year that the Kruses moved in after Thomas had finished medical school. Their son Jeff remembers his father explaining to him and his brother, Chris, that this was a neighborhood that had black and white people in it. Jeff said that once he "became exposed to it, it became part of your thought process." The Jacksons got involved right away. Carolyn became chair of the Education Committee, and Thomas became chairperson of the Housing Committee.

Chris McGuire was house hunting since her husband, Richard, was finishing a tour in Germany and soon would be leaving the service. They bought their home on Fifty-first Street in 1973, "lucked into it," according to Chris, as they had not heard the Sherman Park story. Shortly after moving in, Chris met Judy McBride, and they became "instant friends." They both had two young boys the same age and lived within blocks of each other. From the very first month, the McGuires found it easy to get involved in the neighborhood.

Sherman Park continued to attract new residents. Howard Karsh moved from Glendale to Sherman Park in 1973. Karsh wanted to be able to walk on the Sabbath to Beth Jehudah, the Orthodox congregation led by Rabbi Twerski. Most Jews in Milwaukee were moving to Glendale and suburbs in the north, and the movers asked Karsh if there was some mistake about this move to Fifty-first Boulevard.

In 1974, the *Milwaukee Journal* received a letter from a Merrill resident who described herself as being from "unprogressive and not-with-it-Merrill," asking for a follow-up article about the McBrides. In Huston's article responding to this query, Judy spoke proudly about their five-bedroom home and the rhubarb cake and dish of chopped liver that neighbors had brought when they moved in. They touted Sherman Park as a good place to live.

Jeff and Mary McCreary moved into their roomy house at 2419 North Forty-first Street on June 15, 1975. Their four-bedroom home was priced right for them (although it needed a new roof). It gave their seven-year-old son, Chris, plenty of room. Mary remembers that most of their neighbors were "pretty welcoming" to their new African American neighbors. However, when the white elderly homeowners, residents of the block for decades, moved out within a few years, they rented their homes out and the neighborhood turned more transient.

The McCrearys liked their neighborhood with its racially mixed couples because the people were "pretty open minded," Mary recalled. She had grown up in an all-white neighborhood and wanted her children to live in a diverse and integrated neighborhood. The McCrearys became good friends with the Sutphens who lived behind them and especially enjoyed being part of the annual Grant Boulevard block party.

Thirty-eighth Street block party. *Seated:* unknown, unknown, unknown, Evette McCoy, Rose Coleman, unknown. *Standing:* unknown, unknown, Denise Davis, unknown, Gayna Body. *Courtesy of Tieg Whaley-Smith.*

Pat Geenen, Dave Pearson, Paul Geenen and Gary Glynn enjoy a beer at a Grant Boulevard block party in 1978. *Courtesy of Bill Rumpf.*

Magnolia Verser, a mother of five girls and a boy, moved to Milwaukee from Tennessee in 1952 and bought her home on Thirty-eighth Street in 1976. Verser did not find people very friendly and remembers how whites "walking past" her would not look her in the eye. Verser's mother commented, "People don't do that here." "No one would speak to you," Verser recalled, after she had moved into her new home. There was not a lot of contact between Verser and her white neighbors. "You speak, and sometimes they would not speak," Verser explained. Her kids became good friends with the children of an interracial couple on Thirty-seventh Street. The diversity in Sherman Park did not have much of an impact on Verser's family, and they did not participate in Sherman Park Community Association events. Verser was selective in which white families she socialized with on her block. Her daughter was a close friend of Kay Dee Whaley, the Brazilian adopted daughter of a neighborhood couple with five children from diverse backgrounds. Kay Dee was often at Verser's home, where she was treated as a member of the family, according to Verser.

Herman and Anita Thompson toured a home for sale on Grant Boulevard on a cold and blustery day in March 1977. Classical music was playing at low volume on the record player, a fire was crackling in the fireplace and the price was right. Anita commented, "It was God looking out for us," saying he had put them in this house. Joan Sattler, one of their new neighbors, brought over a plate of cookies when they moved in. The Thompsons fell in love with the house and the community. Anita remembers that she "could come out on her porch and soon there would be a crowd of people."

Other families looking for diversity were attracted to Sherman Park. In 1977, Kathy and Frank Mulvey purchased their beautiful Arts and Crafts–style bungalow on Grant Boulevard. They had moved from Thirty-eighth and Roosevelt where they, along with Tony and Agnes Becker and Barbara Truit, had helped organize a neighborhood group called Capital Neighbors. They had "truly lost on the block busting issue," Kathy recalls. They had done lots of testing and worked with the Fair Housing Council, but their white neighbors had moved out, leaving the "very disheartened" Mulveys behind. They wanted their four children to experience a racially mixed neighborhood and had heard good things about Sherman Park from Pete Mazurek, a member of St. Catherine's Social Concerns Committee and one of the founders of SPCA.

THE PARTIES

The diverse community that attracted new families was strengthened with storied block parties. The LeBlancs moved to their home on Grant Boulevard in 1976, looking for diversity and appreciating the convenience of being able to walk to the Kohl's Food Store, where they could get all the things they needed. Their block was full of kids and his son, David, enjoyed many new friends. The block parties on the 2900 block of Grant Boulevard were legendary. The LeBlancs hosted beignet parties in their backyard on Saturday mornings in the summer. "Every time we did it, it was a beautiful day," Larry recalls.

James and Susan Gramling moved to Grant Boulevard in 1977, attracted both by the diversity of the neighborhood and the fact that Susan Gramling's brother, Larry Siewert, lived on Fifty-first Boulevard. James said this was the first neighborhood where he felt a "common bond and spirit of adventure with everyone who lived there."

The 2400 block of Grant Boulevard block was an "island," the Mulveys said, with memorable parties. After closing off the street, the kids would take their bikes and big wheels out to race. Walter Roob ran a homemade zip line from his garage, and the kids and adults would take turns sliding down the cable. Everyone came out for the annual summer block party, Halloween trick-or-treating and the Christmas parties. These were opportunities for neighbors to "relax and enjoy each other," Gramling said.

In 1978, both the Nervigs and the Hintzs moved to the same block on Grant Boulevard. Rolf and Mary Nervig thought that they would never be able to afford the house that was owned by a Lutheran pastor. But the Nervigs were patient and waited a year before purchasing their house from the pastor with the proceeds from the sale of their house in Wauwatosa. The Nervigs had adopted interracially and were looking for "comfortable, informal mentoring," Mary said. The diversity of the neighborhood and the chance to be with people who shared their values attracted them to Sherman Park. The five families near their home and on Forty-fourth Street became their closest friends. The Nervigs felt part of a group of "pioneers" raising diverse families. Mary recounted the time their daughter Rachael realized that there were "families that are different than us, families where everyone matches."

There were always things going on at Martin and Sandy Hintz's home on Grant. Their son Steven Hintz got his head stuck in one of the columns of the Rogness' house across the street, and the fire department was called.

Matt Nervig and Katie Hintz all dressed up and ready to go (1978). *Courtesy of Steve Hintz.*

Liquid detergent was used to free him, and the porch pillar was saved. Molly, the Hintz's big Irish water spaniel, would jump over their backyard fence when teased by passing kids. Molly would lead Martin on a wild chase through Sherman Park. Martin, a published writer, said that their home was the "Grant Salon," where authors visited and shared experiences. One Jewish storyteller with a huge beard particularly stood out.

The Hintz's St. Patrick's Day party was one of the precursors to Irish Fest, today one of Milwaukee's most popular ethnic festivals. Ireland was in unrest at this time, and Irish musicians were traveling around the states and often stayed with the Hintzes when they were in Milwaukee. The musicians were starved, and when Sandy would bake a ham, "it would last five minutes!" They paid for their room and board with their music. The ten-member bagpipe band warmed up in Sherman Park, marched to the Hintzes' home, up their front steps and finished their piece in the Hintzes' living room. The entire neighborhood joined the party.

There were more fun events. On New Years Eve, all the "Sherman Parkies" would fill a Number 30 bus and take a free bus ride downtown.

A day at the circus. *Front row, left to right:* Steve Hintz, Paul Hoffman, Sarah Rogness, Brian Beaudet, Amy Beaudet, Becky Rogness, David Rogness and Dan Hintz. *Back row:* Sandy Hintz, Katie Hintz (in Sandy's arms), (unknown) Erdman, Peter Rogness and Gerry Rogness (1977). *Courtesy of Steve Hintz.*

People skied to the Geenen's house for a New Years Eve party after a big snowstorm struck. Eva Rumpf, a New Orleans native, was famous for her summer shrimp boil.

The Sherman Park baby-sitting co-op was popular with parents. Points were earned by sitting and spent when, for example, a couple celebrated date night. People took their turns being secretary and kept point balances in a notebook. "This was not a social thing," Mary Nervig recalls. "It was vetted by people that we knew." A popular strategy for building up points was to fill one's house with neighborhood children.

People with musical skills lived in the neighborhood. Dr. Seymour Lefco and his wife, Rachael, lived on the 2900 block of Grant Boulevard in a Mediterranean-style home with a mulberry bush, the berries of which were greatly enjoyed by the kids. Lefco gave free dental care to traveling African American jazz musicians, and neighbors enjoyed going to his house for his jazz piano concerts.

Music from a street musician playing the saxophone in Sherman Park would drift over the block during the summer. The kids played for hours in the wading pool and the big sand box in the park. On the Fourth of July, the kids trimmed their bikes and big wheels and joined the parade to the pavilion where VFW volunteers handed out ice cream cups.

Martin Hintz recalls looking out their kitchen window and watching a park worker on very cold nights hosing down the skating rink. The park's spotlights outlined the bundled worker as he sprayed water and made a tilted and bumpy ice rink that the kids enjoyed.

SPCA

By 1975, SPCA had grown to the point where it could afford an office, using its first United Way grant of $23,000 to open an office at 4634 West Burleigh. The next year, United Way increased the grant to $40,000, allowing them to hire three staff people to support SPCA's seven hundred members. In 1977, SPCA's Sherman Park Plan received a $400,000 Community Block Grant from the City of Milwaukee to fund a training program that enabled women and minorities, supervised by union building tradespeople, to gain the skills needed to get a job in the building trade. Sherman Park Plan crews provided free labor to elderly homeowners, while the owner was responsible for the cost of the building materials. The Sherman Park Plan repaired an average of forty-five to fifty homes every year, with the average age of the owners being seventy-one and average income being $6,400 over the next eight years. This enabled low-income residents like Rachel Adams, who purchased her duplex with HUD financing in Sherman Park in 1978, to maintain her home. The Sherman Park Plan painted her home, repaired her garage, updated her porch, fixed her windows and upgraded her plumbing.

According to an article in the November 1986 SPCA newsletter, the Sherman Park Plan used more than $2 million dollars in block grant funds to rehabilitate homes and train thirty-one women and minority apprentices. Twenty of these workers found employment and four finished their apprenticeship in the building trade and earned journeymen licenses.

The Sherman Park Plan was incorporated as a separate entity, called the Sherman Park Redevelopment Corporation (SPRC) in 1986. As the size of the rehabilitation effort grew, it became difficult for the goals of SPCA to be

Gary Glynn was one of the founding members of the Sherman Park Plan and the Sherman Park Redevelopment Corporation. His background in construction was key to the success of these programs. *Courtesy of Paul Geenen.*

managed along with the goals of the SPRC. Separate entities gave boards and staff of both organizations flexibility in reaching their disparate goals. SPRC worked with local lending institutions to purchase, rehabilitate and sell homes to low-income buyers. It started with four houses but found it very difficult to do more than a few homes at a time. This was a precursor to Habitat for Humanity, which has a successful formula that provides housing to low-income people. Habitat requires five hundred hours of the homeowner's labor in the construction of a new home and uses volunteer workers to build its homes.

It took a tremendous amount of volunteer involvement to negotiate with SPCA's government representatives at the city, county, state and federal levels over issues such as racial steering, segregated schools, the cleared freeway land and the need to maintain the neighborhood's housing stock. Solutions were discussed at weekly meetings, some going until 10:00 p.m., at the homes of the Conways, Gramlings, Jacksons, Johannsens, Lefcos, Sutphens and Sattlers. Education Committee members attended the long, evening school board meetings and wrote position papers that were circulated for comment. Marilyn Johannsen recalls that these activities had an effect on her family, with her daughter saying, "I really know what you are doing is important, but I wish you spent more time at home."

SPCA members caught people's attention, and it was not always positive. The Expressway Committee of SPCA was very good at turning out people at public hearings in 1976 and '77. Downtown businessman George Watts said that SPCA members were "intimidating and effective." Carolyn Jackson, Education Committee chairperson, recalls that School Superintendent Lee McMurrin "did not like them very much."

Joan Sattler was threatened on Sherman Boulevard after a school board meeting when driving home. A driver drove right next to her in the next lane and then again stopped next to her at the light and made some threatening moves. Joan circled around the block before returning to her home. Another time, Ryan Sattler was addressing Milwaukee Public School Board members about the need to integrate grade and junior high schools when he heard clicking of boots. Two young men dressed in khaki tan uniforms with a black armband carrying the swastika insignia were standing behind Sattler trying to create a disturbance. At the time, such disruptions were tolerated at school board meetings. For days, these men hung around the Sattlers' house, their garage was tagged and they received threatening notes with messages made of letters cut from magazines.

Mordecai Lee canvased Sherman Park in the summer of 1976 when he was running for State Assembly. He found predominantly African American families living east of Sherman Boulevard and few living in the section west of Sherman. He remembers being "amazed and ashamed" at the racist comments people made at some of the doors. SPCA members had a lot of work to do to bring their community together.

Sherman Park residents were successful community political activists in the period from 1970 to 1977. SPCA's fight to stop the freeways started in 1970, and victory was declared at the end of 1977. Housing testers gathered evidence that would be used in court, drawing on the experience of National Neighbors and then the Metropolitan Fair Housing Council. SPCA won a lawsuit against four local real estate companies in 1977. The Education Committee started by addressing the segregation in the neighborhoods' two middle schools and, after the ruling to integrate the Milwaukee Public Schools in 1976, put forth a plan to integrate the city's public schools. SPCA's mission of building a community in the Fifth Ward with a high quality of life, quality education and beautiful homes got pretty complicated!

CHAPTER 3
DAVID AND GOLIATH

"It was all cooked and dried. Mind your own business; stay home and mind the kids."
Surveyor's response when homeowner Cindy Cukor questioned clearance for the freeway.
—Richard Cutler's *Greater Milwaukee's Growing Pains*

Sherman Park Opposes the Park West Freeway

The German autobahn network impressed President Dwight D. Eisenhower while he served as the supreme commander of the Allied forces in World War II. He signed the bill authorizing the construction of a freeway system to connect the nations' existing highways in 1956. By 1967, the North–South Freeway (I-43) and the East–West Freeway (I-94) were under construction and connecting routes were being planned to tie the system together. Suburbs, with new homes on large lots close to trendy shopping centers, were springing up around Milwaukee. Milwaukee's streets were getting congested, and suburbanites wanted to shorten their commuting time to their jobs in the city. The freeway system was seen as a solution to these problems.

Milwaukee's pattern of housing and school segregation, compounded by white flight, caused entire blocks to turn over, changing from homeowners who had lived there for years and took great pride in maintaining their homes to a transitional rental population that did not have the skills nor resources to keep up the properties they were living in.

The quality of life in Sherman Park was being drastically affected by the construction of the freeways, the segregation of schools and the harsh real estate practices. It was no accident that the first three standing SPCA committees were Expressway, Housing and Education. SPCA's newsletter kept neighborhood residents informed on how to get involved.

In 1971, Walter Johannsen published an article in the Sherman Park community newsletter opposing the freeway. The clearing of the freeway land was causing real estate panic in surrounding neighborhoods, and there were racial undertones in the siting of the freeways. Those who wished to avoid driving through the central city found expressways to be a quick egress.

The Park West Freeway, extending from the Marquette Interchange to Sherman Boulevard, would greatly increase traffic on Sherman Boulevard. Freeway opponents believed that once the Park West was built, a freeway segment called the "Gap Closer" would then be built down Sherman Boulevard, extending north and connecting to the freeway segment that feeds onto Fond du Lac Avenue at Sixty-eighth and Hampton (Highway 145). The North–South Freeway (I-43) on the east, the "Gap Closer" on the west and the Park West Freeway on the south would isolate West Side businesses, churches and schools.

Many of Milwaukee's influential people supported building freeways. In 1970, Milwaukee's Common Council, the county board, the county executive, labor unions, the area's three television stations and the *Milwaukee Journal* all supported the construction of the Park West Freeway, Walter Johannsen said in his 1992 interview. Most of the Southeast Wisconsin Regional Planning Commission (SEWRPC), the planning entity for seven counties in southeastern Wisconsin, thought freeway opponents were "little more than noisy, single-issue radicals," according to Richard Cutler in *Growing Pains*.

George Watts, a prominent downtown businessman and a member of SEWRPC, said that people were "wedded to their automobiles" and that freeways were critical to the success of downtown Milwaukee. He was also dismissive of community groups, saying "community groups are valuable even if they are wrong" and "Sherman Park can make mistakes."

SPCA mobilized its members and turned them out in large numbers at SEWRPC public hearings. They joined the Westside Citizens Coalition, an organization of ten community groups opposing freeways; entered a lawsuit asking for an environmental study; and requested that the construction of the freeway be temporarily halted.

In 1972, the anti-freeway forces in the entire city mounted candidates for thirteen of the twenty-five county board positions, with eight being elected, according to Richard Cutler in *Growing Pains*. That same year, Federal Judge John Reynolds ruled in favor of the Westside Citizens Coalition, saying that an environmental statement had to be written before the freeway could be built. Congressman Henry Reuss assigned one of his staff, Mordecai Lee, to work with the people from Sherman Park.

It was thought that Ryan Sattler, as a businessman, would be more credible with the press, and he was chosen to be the group's spokesperson. Sattler said, "We were pretty green, in our mid-twenties," but he stood in front of the TV cameras and read a statement that "they had worked on for days," announcing that they were taking Milwaukee County to federal court over the need for an environmental study. The next day, while at work, Sattler got a call from Herb Kohl, CEO of Kohl's Food Stores, saying, "What the hell were you doing on TV yesterday!" Herb Kohl became very supportive of the group's efforts.

A majority of Milwaukee's citizens supported the freeways, but a number of elected officials had reservations. A referendum had passed on November 5, 1974, approving the building of five new freeway segments, with 52.4 percent in favor and 48 percent opposed. In 1975, Congressman Reuss published a position paper opposing the freeways and became the first public official to do so. He soon was joined by a new generation of political leaders that emerged out of the movement opposing the freeways, including John Norquist, Jim Moody and Mordecai Lee, who were all elected to the state assembly. State representatives Barbara Ulichey and Dennis Conta were also members of the legislative team that fought the building of freeways through Milwaukee.

On May 13, 1975, John C. Geilfuss, chairman of the Metropolitan Milwaukee Association Chamber of Commerce (MMAC), and George Watts spoke in favor of the freeways at a four-hour public hearing on the environmental statement. Many residents at this hearing opposed the freeways. Richard Cutler was appointed chairperson of a committee to resolve the impasse. It was called the "6-6-6 Committee" because its membership consisted of six members for the freeway, six against and six who were "neutral." The committee voted twelve to six to continue freeway construction, but their vote had no impact, according to Cutler.

The first breakthrough, Lee recalled in a 2012 interview, was when Reuss's office identified an obscure ruling that each segment had to be justified individually with its own environmental impact statement, a concept called "segmentation." The low traffic projected on the Park West segment could be used to stop the project.

Eighteen legislators from the Milwaukee metropolitan area sent a letter dated January 3, 1977, to Governor Pat Lucy, asking him to stop the construction of the southern leg of the stadium freeway. People were becoming alarmed by the large number of homes that were being destroyed, "cutting a trough through some fairly stable neighborhoods," according to Bill Drew, an alderman for the City of Milwaukee at the time. People were concerned about the impact on their neighborhoods, the forced relocation of residents, the high-quality housing that was being destroyed and the properties taken off the tax rolls.

The tipping point in the fight against the freeway occurred late in the summer of 1977. A group of freeway opponents worked with UWM professors for the entire summer scrutinizing SEWRPC's rationale for the construction of the freeway system. They uncovered the fact that Chris Bauer, the head of the state's DOT, was planning for Level A service at rush hour, meaning that people would be able to move through the city at posted highway speeds during rush hour. Freeway opponents published a report making the case that Level A traffic flow was not needed at rush hour and that a lower level of service would be much better for the city residents. They called this level of service "creative congestion," according to Mordecai Lee.

Convincing everyone that all of the planned freeways did not have to be built was a long process. Lee ran and won a seat in the State Assembly, saying he would "kill the Park West Freeway." But the freeway had many lives and would consume ten years of his political career. He said that he "thought he understood government, but when the entire bureaucracy is going in one direction, there are a million doorways you have to go through to change that direction. Killing the Park West Freeway was one of the proudest moments in my political career."

The strong case against Level A service at rush hour forced the *Milwaukee Journal* to change its editorial position on the freeways. The freeway construction program was finally stopped on December 28, 1977, when SEWRPC reversed itself and voted ten to seven that the Park West Freeway and the "Gap Closer" would not be built. It had taken ten years and numerous voting victories to overcome the entrenched highway lobby.

In 1977, Governor Pat Lucy appointed members to a Park West Freeway Task Force to develop plans for the vacant land. Lee Sherman Dreyfus was elected governor in 1978, and he signed the bill abolishing the Milwaukee County Expressway Commission. This was "the last gasp of the highway lobby," according to Lee. Jerry Schwerm, an anti-freeway advocate, became head of Milwaukee County Department of Public Works, effectively ending the state/county project.

Sherman Park residents were overjoyed. Johannsen called the stopping of the freeway one of his proudest moments. The Park West Task Force, led by David Hoh, started working on a new plan for the vacant land, which was co-owned by the county and the state. SPCA called its first planning meeting for the vacant freeway land on February 17, 1977.

Housing Discrimination

Block busting in Sherman Park was "very serious," Marilyn Johannsen said. Realtors placed multiple "for sale" signs on a corner house to make it look like the adjacent houses were also on the market. The wall-to-wall signage made it feel like the entire street was for sale. White flight was forcing property values down. Realtors sent mailers and placed door hangers on homes, stating that a family with numerous children had moved in just down the block and that the value of each home was never going to be worth as much again.

Magnolia Verser moved to Sherman Park in 1976 and joined three African Americans families already living on Thirty-eighth Street. Verser said, "People started moving out," and soon there were no white families on the block.

An insurance agent wrote, "Minorities were encroaching" on the Thompson's home insurance application in 1977, according to Anita Thompson.

The Board of Realtors asked Sattler, president of SPCA, to leave, not giving him time to finish his presentation. Appraisal manuals had "strongly negative racial references" before 1977, according to Juliet Saltman in *A Fragile Movement*.

Edward and Theresa Valent, an interracial couple, bought a duplex on the corner of Fortieth and Locust in 1976. They wanted to be near St. Catherine's, as they thought their children would go to school there. Edward was quite sure they were "steered," as white couples were being shown homes west of Sherman Boulevard, and they were shown homes east of the boulevard. In 1977 or 1978, the Valents were turned down for a home repair loan by First Wisconsin, even though the loan had a 50 percent guarantee by the city, their combined income was more than adequate and Edward knew the loan officer personally. The Valents changed banks.

Many African Americans wanted to move from the overcrowded housing in the central city to the larger homes in Sherman Park. In 1970, most African Americans men had factory jobs, leading the nation with 73.4 percent employment, according to a 2012 *Milwaukee Journal* article. In 1970, Milwaukee's factories were operating at their peak, and with stable incomes, these workers could purchase homes.

Some Sherman Park residents were supportive of African Americans moving into their neighborhood. The Housing Committee of SPCA outlined the double goals to "eliminate illegal discriminatory and destructive housing practices and to maintain and improve the quality of the housing stock," according to Gregory Squires in *Sherman Park*. SPCA supported the 1972 ordinance proposed by Aldermen Warren Braun and John Kalwitz prohibiting the use of "for sale" signs by realtors.

From the beginning of SPCA, concern was raised about how to integrate Sherman Park uniformly. The section to the east of Sherman Boulevard was predominately black and low income while the area to west was predominately white and middle class. There was little participation in SPCA activities by the renters in the eastern section. The Housing Committee, under James Gramling, found funds to promote economic and racial diversity by recruiting black and white renters receiving rent assistance to integrate the eastern and western sections of Sherman Park. The good schools and affordable rents were a strong draw.

In 1976, SPCA received a $15,000 grant from the Ford Foundation for a staff person for the Neighborhood Affirmative Marketing Program. The staff person met with tenants who attended the city's rent assistance program orientation sessions and recruited tenants to integrate either the east or west section of Sherman Park, depending on the tenant's race. The goal was racial and economic integration while avoiding a concentration of low-income families in any part of Sherman Park. The program was quite successful, with twenty-nine families locating in Sherman Park, half of these being pro-integration moves, in its first year. Unfortunately, the original staff person moved out of state, and her replacement was not as successful. The funding ended, and the program was dropped.

Lawn mower. *Courtesy of Jim Wend.*

Sherman Park residents fought the racial steering being carried out by the real estate industry. First Joe Battles of National Neighbors and later the Metropolitan Fair Housing Council trained Sherman Park residents as housing testers. Black, white and mixed pairs, perfectly matched as far as income, education, the number of children and the kind of houses they were looking for, toured homes on the market on the West Side. One couple followed the next within an hour, and tape recorders were used to document the treatment received from the realtors.

Sharon and Skip Seager were surprised by the racial discrimination they uncovered when they participated as testers, they said in a 1992 interview. The testing was "real fun, real sixties stuff," Carol Holton recalled in her 1992 interview. Large numbers of African Americans volunteered for testing. "White people and black people were shown different areas of the city, based on their race," Edward Valent said in his 1992 interview.

Theresa Valent, who was a testing trainer, said people returned, saying, "I don't think you will find anything." The realtors were "nice but very covert," Theresa said. The discrimination was clear when you compared the treatment the test couples received. Theresa said that this experience "did something to her," and she could not be a tester because it upset her too much.

Jeff and Mary McCreary, both African American testers, were victims of racial steering. Jeff appreciated SPCA's efforts, saying in a 2012 interview, "They were trying to maintain Sherman Park as a safe place to live, (with) diversity, all that good stuff." The McCrearys shook off the discrimination they received when they attempted to purchase a home in Washington Highlands, an area with larger, more expensive homes than those in Sherman Park. Their son Chris felt strongly about his parent's experience, though, saying in a 2012 interview, "If my parents were not discriminated against, I would have grown up in the Washington Highland area."

In 1977, the Supreme Court ruled that testing could be used as evidence against real estate companies. In May of that same year, SPCA filed a lawsuit with the U.S. Department of Housing and Urban Development against Town Realty, Wauwatosa Realty, Keske Realty and Relocation Realty. The complaint was based on forty-two testing visits made by black and white home buyers during a fourteen-month period, according to Juliet Saltman in *A Fragile Movement*. Some of the firms closed, and the rest of them settled. The McCrearys and other members of the suit received cash settlements. This was another win for SPCA. "We had such credibility, (with) this very professional newsletter…press releases, but we were not as big as our audience thought," Sattler said in a 2012 interview.

THE EAGLES

In October 1976, Sherman Park residents Gary Glynn and Paul Geenen, both parents of adoptive, interracial families, attempted to join the Eagles Club to play handball. This was the fraternal club the NAACP Youth Council had picketed in 1966. The men found sponsors and were questioned at a pre-induction interview to make sure that they were not members of the Communist Party, that they believed in God and they were willing to pledge allegiance to the U.S. flag.

Glynn and Geenen were not accepted into the auditorium to be received by the membership. An Eagle representative put his arm around Geenen's shoulder and said, "Sometimes members vote to turn down candidates." The men attributed their rejection to an article about the Glynn family and two other interracial families that had run earlier in February.

Attorney Steve Glynn filed a case on a pro-bono basis with Dennis Conta, secretary of state of the Wisconsin Department of Revenue. Testimony at the hearing confirmed the fact that Glynn and Geenen had been kept together through the interview process and that a separate vote had been taken on the two men. At that vote, some members cast a black ball, meaning that the two men's request for membership was denied.

In May 1978, the Wisconsin Department of Revenue removed the Eagles tax exemptions. The Eagles closed in spring 1988, and the building now houses the Rave, which the younger set flocks to, featuring live music and webcasts by national music groups.

The Schools

The Milwaukee Public Schools Board had been practicing "intact busing" since 1957. This practice called for students to be segregated by race, resulting in African American children in overcrowded schools being bused to schools with available space but still being kept in separate, segregated classrooms in the receiving school. The African American students were even bused home sometimes for lunch to avoid having black and white students eating together. Twenty-two of the Milwaukee Public Schools were predominantly African American, with fourteen of these schools having 90 percent black student bodies. In July 1965, Lloyd Barbee, representing the NAACP, filed a claim in Federal Court asking that Milwaukee Public Schools be desegregated. In 1966, the School Board declared that desegregating the schools was impossible due to the city's segregated housing.

In the early 1970s, Sherman Park residents were active in supporting neighborhood schools as they played a big part in making the area a good place to raise a family. Schools were struggling to maintain a stable student population. Some whites were pulling their children out of schools perceived as being predominately black and moving them to schools that were thought to have white student populations.

An integrated crowd of parents and children protest against the practice of "intact busing." The sign "Integration Works," strapped to the large dog, later became very popular in Sherman Park (1976). *Courtesy of Milwaukee County Historical Museum.*

"Integration works" sign in Sherman Park at Rumpf home on Fifty-third Street. Jerre Wisneski, Margaret Rumpf, Andrew Rump, Timothy Rumpf, Hillary (unknown), Heather (unknown), Robbie Grunwald (1976). *Courtesy of Bill Rumpf.*

Families had a lot of school choices on where to send their children. MPS schools included Thirty-eighth Street, Townsend, Fifty-first, Steuben, Peckham (all junior high schools) and Washington High School. Parochial schools included St. Catherine's, St. Anne's, St. Thomas's and Mount Calvary Lutheran, Pius High and Alverno.

Only 29 percent of the children at Thirty-eighth Street School were passing the standardized tests. Peckham Junior High School (which became Jack Robinson) was black, and Steuben, located a little over a mile away, (which became HiMount) Junior High School was white. Both were feeder schools for Washington High School, which was 65–70 percent white. In 1973, Thirty-eighth Street and Townsend were integrated but turning black.

The SPCA Education Committee organized over the need to integrate the two middle schools, Peckham and Steuben, feeding Washington High School. As soon as a school became 20 percent black, whites fled and the school turned all black, Judy McBride said.

SPCA's Education Committee, with a range of six to fifteen members, had a much larger effect on Milwaukee Public Schools than their size would suggest. The SPCA Education Committee members were part of a citywide group that worked to improve things at both Peckham and Steuben Junior High Schools and Washington High Schools. The names of these advocacy groups changed over time, starting as the Peckham-Steuben Committee and evolving into Citizens United for Education. These were important initiatives that made significant changes, such as bringing the computer technology specialty program to Washington.

Lila Kelly, with her distinctive voice, honed in countless school board meetings, was an influential member of SPCA's Education Committee. The Kellys' efforts in advocating for their daughter, Grace, was the inspiration behind the 1972 groundbreaking state law that ensured that every child with disabilities in Wisconsin was guaranteed an equal education. The Kellys were passionate advocates for children with disabilities. Jerome Brandl, principal of Washington High School, describes Lila Kelly as one who "would scorch the board anytime they don't take into account the needs of exceptional children."

Although the SPCA Education Committee was a small group, it researched issues carefully and was "always listened to," according to Nicholas Scaeve, a member of the committee from 1974 to 1978. A member of the committee attended every school board meeting, and Superintendent Lee R. McMurrin knew all the committee members by name.

In November 1976, Federal Judge John Reynolds ruled that the Milwaukee Public School system had to be desegregated. SPCA's Education Committee developed a plan for a citywide integrated school system using data supplied by Mike Barndt of the UWM Urban Affairs Department. The Education Committee proposed integrated, pie-shaped districts covering both city and adjacent suburbs that would share the busing burden equally between the races.

"It was very, very exciting, everyone was revved up…(feeling) very hopeful," Judy McBride recalled. "We were feeling so empowered…MPS district people came to Marion's (McEvilly) house to hear our plan." Sherman Park was the only school district, out of twenty-eight in the city, that advocated for integration, Tom McGinnity said. McGinnity, a member of SPCA's Education Committee, was later appointed the MPS Community Superintendent for the area.

The court rejected the citywide integration plan that called for busing both white and black students, Susan Gramling noted in her 1992 interview. Instead, a citywide specialty school system that attracted students from both races was implemented. Lila Kelly was one of the representatives on the Committee of 100 that played a significant role in creating the plan for specialty schools. Dr. Lee McMurren's concept was for each school to develop a specialty that would encourage parents to desegregate the school system voluntarily.

Howard Karsh felt that "Jews moved out of Sherman Park as a reaction when MPS dummied down the curriculum. It was not fear but a desire for better education." However, Alan Borsuk describes the Jewish families moving to the northern suburbs as part of a wider trend of people being attracted by the suburban lifestyle. The people in Sherman Park had tremendous impact on reversing this trend. As Judy McBride pointed out, "There were only thirty of us, but they thought we have three hundred!" Lila Kelly became so well known on school issues that MPS gave her a special desk in the central office, according to Carolyn Jackson in a 2012 interview.

Thirty-eighth School became one of the most successful specialty schools in the neighborhood because of the way its staff, parents and students worked together. It was one of the first schools in Milwaukee to use the

Election night! *From left to right, front row:* Peggy Kenner, Marian McEvilly, Judy McBride and Carol Holton. *Back row:* Carol (unknown), Ilsa Ankel, Peter Stacy, Kay Pena and Lilla Kelly (1975). *Courtesy of Byron McBride.*

Doris Stacy talks to students as a member of the school board. Diana Stacy, Mikle McBride, Jonathan McBride, Doris Stacy and Amy McBride (1977). *Courtesy of Byron McBride.*

open classroom design, where students work in small groups on projects that incorporate reading, math and other subjects. Children visited the library whenever they wanted to work on their reports. After reading and gathering the information, children read back their report to anyone in the building, including the janitor. Once a month, parents would come to view the children's projects.

Emma Jabs, the Thirty-eighth School principal, gave learning coordinators Elaine Stalheim and Foyne Mahaffey complete freedom in creating learning programs for the children. Stalheim and Mahaffey went over the standardized testing and focused on the areas where the children needed help. This moved the scores of students passing standardized tests from 29 percent to 90 percent. Stalheim and Mahaffey toured other schools and recruited the best teachers for Thirty-eighth.

Stalheim, who became principal when Emma Jabs retired, said in a 2012 interview, "What…made the school go…was a circle, parents who cared about the neighborhood and wanted a multicultural experience for their children, our students and the participation of the community." African Americans were confident that things were going to change for the better in their school. The police often would question her as to why she would request only one officer for an open house of five hundred people. Neighbors and Sherman Park people worked together to make the school a better place for their children. "Sherman Park people were not just do-gooders, they were (comfortably) multi-cultural," Stalheim said.

The Exceptional Education teacher at Thirty-eighth School, Mark Luebke, smoothly integrated his students into the mainstream classes. The students were not seen as being different. Students moved easily throughout the school; lines, to use the rest rooms, for example, were seen as a waste of time and avoided at all costs, and each teacher set their own protocol for bathroom trips.

When Jerome Brandl became principal of Washington High School in 1971, the perception in the white community was that Marshall High School, at Sixty-fourth and Capital, was the "white" high school and Washington was the "black" high school. White parents stood in long lines at Marshall at 5:00 a.m. on enrollment day. By 1975 or '76, Washington High School's student population would increase from 2,300 to 2,800, with the percentage of black students increasing every year.

In 1970, there had been serious racial incidents at Washington High School. Jerome Brandl set up an informal advisory committee to reflect the diversity of Sherman Park. White students coming from the segregated

First day of school. *From left to right:* Steve Hintz, David Rogness and Brian Beaudet (1982). *Courtesy of Steve Hintz First Day of School.*

Steuben Junior High School at Fifty-second Street felt threatened, and the black students coming from Peckham at Thirty-sixth Street did not feel safe either. This was the first time for many to interact with students who were not of their own race.

Brandl, in his 1996 interview, said that integrating school activities was very difficult. As an example, he cited the cheerleading situation. The cheerleading team was white because the senior cheerleaders were selecting their younger friends for the team. Practice was first thing in the morning, which was convenient for the cheerleaders who lived nearby but not for the African Americans who wanted to join the team, as they came to school on the bus. This was changed to have adults make the selection of cheerleaders, but this did not please anyone. If there were multiple candidates for prom queens and class officers and all candidates were black and one was white, all the whites would vote for the white candidate. People were often upset, and protests were common. Black History Month in February caused tensions between the two groups, with students making comments such as, "Well, why don't we have a German History program?"

In 1982, Washington High School started a specialty computer program with the support of the school district, desegregation funds, Northwestern Mutual Life Insurance and St. Joseph's Hospital. Neighborhood children, including the Mulvey children, enjoyed taking summer computer classes.

The Kellys' daughter, Judy, and Nancy Walch, who later became a swim coach at UWM, were part of a four-member girl's swimming team that was practicing in the swimming pool located in the basement of the high school. "These young ladies were so fantastic that they competed against some of the best talent in the city and won," said their coach, Robert Sivak, in a 1996 interview. The water was frigid, there were only two lanes and each lane was one-sixth the length of a standard high school swimming pool.

In 1977, one of Washington High School's members of the boys' swim team was shot in a fight outside the North Central YMCA at Twelfth and Teutonia. The SPCA Education Committee developed a plan for a new pool at Washington High School, using federal funds. A.O. Smith offered to fly the documents to Washington, D.C., if members of SPCA paid for the fuel. The bill was taken to Washington, D.C., and included in a funding passed by Congress before the Christmas recess. The new pool, complete with warm water and a platform for people with disabilities, opened in February 1984.

Lee recalled those times in a 2012 interview, describing it as a time when "the world was our oyster and the 'man' was easily identified, i.e. the racist school board, racist realtors and the insensitive political structure." Marilyn Johannsen, in a 2012 interview, said, "You could not depend on your alderman to know what needed to be done," and Johannsen "became accustomed to the fact that you had to work to make things happen."

Stopping the freeway, fighting housing discrimination and creating quality, integrated schools solidified the diverse community that was Sherman Park. Ryan Sattler said, "When you have a victory, just like David over Goliath, you can take on anybody!" SPCA allowed residents to work together to address these issues. The newsletter kept people informed on developments and was an important ingredient. Idealistic residents, working together to share the burden and address these issues, found community. Better yet, children of this community saw their parents being successful, and they grew up feeling that they too were empowered to change things for the better, creating a legacy for the future.

CHAPTER 4

INTEGRATION WORKS!

Careful! Important Articles in here! PLEASE do not "lose". Thank you! Most of the articles in here are about discrimination and people who do something about it!!!!!

—Message on school envelope by Sarah Geenen, age nine

Milwaukee Kickers

Athletics, especially soccer, played a key role in building community in Sherman Park. Neighborhood schools had been replaced by the new magnet schools, eliminating a common place where people had socialized. The Milwaukee Kickers were started in 1968, according to Kathy Geiger, a Kicker's volunteer, and by 1970, leagues had been formed in both Whitefish Bay and Wauwatosa. Residents of Sherman Park, families like the Danahers and the Waltiers, had heard about soccer at Alverno Campus School where their children were enrolled. Judy Sutphen researched the sport at the library, according to her daughter, Mona. In 1970, Geiger's family enjoyed a parent-kid soccer game at a family reunion. Afterward, her six-year-old exclaimed, "I want to play that game!"

A year before the court integration order, some parents on the Eastside of Milwaukee had negotiated with the Milwaukee Public School Board to supply buses to transport their children to Lloyd Street School, which at the time was entirely black. In 1976, Rollie Kohl, one of the parents, created the Lloyd Soccer Region with racially, economically and gender integrated players. Kohl called Judy McBride, saying, "We don't want to be alone!" He asked that a second division with similarly diverse teams be started in Sherman Park. Soccer took off in Sherman Park "like wildfire," Geiger said. Families had their children in a wide number of schools, and soccer replaced the neighborhood schools for bonding the community's families together.

Starting from the Grant Boulevard and Fifty-first Street area, the league quickly grew to encompass the entire Sherman Park area. Rosters were carefully selected to ensure that the teams were balanced racially, by gender, economically and by skill levels. Judy McBride, the league manager, visited games wearing a distinctive hat made out of a split soccer ball, observed coaches and made notes about strong players and those needing more support. McBride, a school psychologist, called herself "the IEP (Individualized Education Program) coach." McBride and Ryan Sattler also promoted Sherman Park's racial, gender and economic team integration at citywide Kicker meetings. In the fall of 2007, McBride was inducted into the Milwaukee Kickers Hall of Fame for her leadership in Kicker soccer.

Soccer was an important experience for those who grew up in Sherman Park. Mikle McBride said in a 2012 interview, "It was the one thing that tied all the families together at a lot of levels." It was important for the parents, because while the kids played, Mom and Dad hung out at the sidelines, discussed community issues and signed petitions. Children growing up in Sherman Park cite their soccer experiences as one of their earliest memories. David Sutphen remembers the "tight cotton shorts and the nylon perforated shirts in bright colors," a far cry from today's baggy uniforms. Ruth Nervig remembers learning to focus and concentrate, starting with "standing in the middle of the field and gazing off," and looking forward to the oranges at the end of the game. Tieg Whaley-Smith remembers riding his bike to join neighborhood families gathering at the field for soccer practice, providing an image of community for him at a young age.

The diverse soccer teams provided the children of Sherman Park some of their first experiences with the segregated world that existed outside of their neighborhood. David Rogness said, "I was struggling to find an identity…as being biracial…the Milwaukee Kickers did it for me." Rogness played teams that were always "more white," with nice shoes and good-looking uniforms. "I remember feeling proud to be a part of this group that was different." Coach David Waltier's Sherman Park Select team beat three Fox Valley

Ingrid (unknown), Kristin Geenen, Pat Geenen and Judy McBride (1979). *Courtesy of Paul Geenen.*

U8 Milwaukee Kickers team. *Front row, left to right:* unknown, unknown, Jamie Danaher, unknown, Dan Hintz, Steven Hintz. *Back row, left to right:* Paul Hoffman, unknown, Margaret Rumpf, unknown, Julie Jackson, Karl Pearson, Mike McCutcheon, Brian Beaudet. Coaches: Dave Pearson, Mike Danaher, Bryan (unknown) (1979). *Courtesy of Karl Pearson-Cater.*

teams, and the team advanced to the state championship. Mikle McBride remembers that their team had the only kids of color on the field at the Green Bay tournament.

The coaches in Sherman Park took great care to make sure the girls had equal playing time. Pearson-Cater spoke about the teams' gender diversity, saying, "The kids from the suburbs, their heads were exploding, because Julie (Jackson) and Margi (Rumpf) were so good." The confidence created by playing on co-ed teams and keeping up with the boys "laid down a foundation of a lifetime of soccer," said Sarah Geenen.

Playing on racially and gender-integrated teams helped to dispel the stereotypes at a young age. Karl Pearson-Cater remembers, at the age of seven, piling into a parent's car to go to soccer practice, and hearing one of the children say, "I don't like black people!" Pearson-Cater, trying to fit in, agreed. His mother, Gretchen Pearson, reminded Pearson-Cater, "Jimmy Kruse is black, and he is your best friend." Pearson-Cater thought about it and then said, "Oh, I guess I like black people!" He describes this incident as an opportunity to "to think through these things. These are dumb, naïve, young conversations (which) my mom cleared… up with reality."

Supportive parents coached the teams, and kids learned to play soccer from a variety of coaches. Later, when Julie Jackson encountered some racism playing soccer in high school, she felt confident enough to brush it off. Kristin Powers remembers fondly that her mother, Patricia Geenen, was her coach. Power's co-ed team stayed together for many years and showcased Sherman Park's philosophy of inclusion.

Sherman Park expanded to four leagues—Mid-City, Sherman Park South, Sherman Park North and Northwest—but gradually shrunk back to one league, Milwaukee West. As the kids aged out of grade schools and

Opposite, top: Sherman Park sweeps U14 division. *Front row, left to right:* Karl Pierson, Steve Au, Matt Wesley, Mikle McBride, Joe Pischette, Brian McGuire, Josh Goldberg and Steve Provan. *Back row, left to right:* Sam Agonzin, Sean Huston, Kevin Van Lannan, Donnie Brown, Jon McBride, Brian Dawson, Chuck Waltier and Sean Owens. Coaches: David Waltier and Byron McBride (1982). *Courtesy of Karl Pearson-Cater.*

Opposite, bottom: U12 Pee Wees Girls Soccer team takes second place at the Elm Grove Annual Memorial Soccer Tournament. *Front row:* Kim Yeo, Maggie Gramling, Margaret Rumpf, Robin Pena, Andrea Davel and Julie Jackson. *Back row:* Roberta Harris, Sandy Siewert, unknown, Amy McBride (coach), Tanya Ingvolstad, Rene Davel and Amy Tesch (1982). *Courtesy of Bill Rumpf.*

entered high schools, the boys played on school teams in the fall and the girls in the spring. This forced the dropping of co-ed teams. There is no agreement on what caused the decline in Sherman Park soccer teams, but McBride attributed it to losing coaches and volunteers when the kids were in high school.

Some continued with soccer into their adult lives. Sarah Geenen played on the University of Chicago team, where she met her husband, whose apartment overlooked the soccer field. She still plays today and is close friends with the women on her league team. Chris McCreary has turned his interest in the sport into a career. He coaches three teams for the FC Milwaukee Nationals, an elite league started by the Milwaukee Kickers with the goal of developing players that can compete at the national level. Soccer carries on to the next generation. All of Kristin Powers's children play soccer, and she coaches her daughter's team. Sarah Geenen said one way that they keep diversity in their lives is the soccer team her son Shanti plays on, where half of the players are Latino.

David Sutphen and Chris McCreary traveled all over the midwest and went to Europe twice while playing for a Bavarian team in their high school years. Sutphen said, "There was no way in the world that he would have gotten into Amherst" without soccer. Today, Sutphen sits on the board of the U.S. Soccer Foundation, the major charitable arm of major-league soccer.

Both Patrick and Mattew McGuire coach soccer and carry on the Sherman Park coaching tradition of actively reaching out to the parents and players. Tieg Whaley-Smith led the effort to get soccer restarted in Sherman Park and now, after just two years, has three teams practicing in the same Washington Park soccer fields that were used by players in 1976. Whaley-Smith's team of eight-year-olds, the mighty Eagles, is just as diverse as the Sherman Park teams thirty-five years ago.

The community, friendship and diversity the children of Sherman Park experienced had a long-term effect on their lives. "These differences can provide the seeds of innovation, progress and understanding," Scott Page says in his book, *The Difference*. Growing up in Sherman Park gave the next generation skills in community building, problem solving and creativity.

Steven Hintz is a film writer, producer and CEO of Simple World Mentoring, an agency that mentors kids on probation. His experience of growing up with diverse friends who did not accept racism, some rich and others poor, gave him a world view that enhanced his formal education and led him to found Simple World Mentoring, providing social services to young people and their families in Arkansas and North Carolina. Hintz has been mentoring youth since 1998, when he founded Peacemakers, Inc. in Milwaukee to serve children of incarcerated parents. Hintz has an appreciation for people who have less.

Ruth Nervig, currently in Senegal, West Africa, where she is working as a Peace Corps volunteer, thinks that growing up with diversity made her aware of injustice and poverty. She lives in a small village, feeling "a sense of unity" with the people who outwardly seem very different. She is surrounded either by Senegalese or the Peace Corps community, the latter of which tends to be white and middle class. Nervig gets "pathetically emotional" when the Senegalese people comment on her race. She is used to be called "white and rich" by the Senegalese and draws on her lifelong experience dealing with complex relations between people of different races. Her Peace Corps experiences give her a clearer picture of "how to live a responsible life."

David Sutphen, managing partner of Brunswick Group's District of Columbia office, an international corporate communication consulting company, writes about his experience growing up in a diverse family in his article "The Whole is Greater Than the Sum of Its Parts" in the *Huffington Post*. "Who you are as a person—from racial identity to your cultural connections—fundamentally drives your belief in and desire to find the common ground among us all." In an interview, Sutphen commented, "Stereotypes don't make sense" if you are an interracial kid.

For example, when Sutphen was a boy, he told his friend Cory Thompson, "I don't like black people." Thompson responded ,"Well dude, your dad is black!" Sutphen said in an interview, "You know first-hand that not all white people are racist because your mom is white and married a black man. And since Dad gets up and goes to work every morning, it can't be true that all black people are lazy and on welfare." Sutphen feels that he is lucky in having learned to navigate "the ever treacherous waters of race and culture in our society." He sees his ability to analyze interactions with others and understand his surroundings as a strength. Sutphen's article was written shortly before Barrack Obama was elected president in November 2008, and he sees Obama as a person who found his diversity to be a strength. Sutphen describes himself as " a unique shade of gray—a blend that reflects dimensions of both."

Memories stand out for the kids who grew up in Sherman Park, and they play a role in how many of them pursue their lives and careers today. Karl Pearson-Carter, senior content architect at Ciceron, a publisher, said that the diversity in Sherman Park seemed normal until he got to UW Eau Claire, which he found to be "very white." Pearson-Carter said that it

The girls get silly. *From left to right, front:* Julie Jackson, Chris Jackson, Joel Ellwanger (center), Kristin Geenen, Candy Waltier and Sarah Geenen. *Rear:* Annette Erdman and Rebecca Rumpf (1977). *Courtesy of Paul Geenen.*

was "interesting to talk to kids from white areas" that were uncomfortable greeting "a black guy walking down the street." Pearson-Carter told his classmates, "If the guy looks tough, is part of a gang and is wearing colors," avoid him. "If the guys look ok, don't be afraid. You need to pick up on other things other than race, to make the decisions."

Kristin Powers, professor of Advanced Studies in Education and Counseling at California State University Long Beach, remembers feeling relieved at being with many multi-racial families in Sherman Park after her family moved from Miami, Florida, where they had experienced racial tension. She and her sister, Sarah, were the only white kids in a summer program in Sherman Park, and the African American children called the sisters "Laverne and Shirley." This taught Powers how it feels to be " a white person in the minority," she said.

Her sister, Sarah Geenen, a research professor in the Regional Research Institute for Human Services at Portland State University, remembers the time in Wisconsin when Native Americans were fighting for fishing rights, and she saw a t-shirt on an auto mechanic in northern Wisconsin that said, "Kill an Indian and save a fish." She learned how unjust racial prejudice can be. Geenen recalled her parents instructing her African American brother about what to do if the police stopped him, just like African American parents had to do. Geenen's husband, Prashant Dubey, grew up in both India and the United States, and their family celebrates both cultures. Geenen says living in a diverse community teaches "the fact that there is more than one way to look at the world."

Jonathan McBride, now on the White House staff in the Personnel Department, said in an article written by the *Milwaukee Journal* columnist Jim Stingle, "Everyone—individuals, organizations, corporations, politicians—struggles to understand an increasingly diverse America. It has helped immensely to have lived it." McBride's sister, Amy, an administrator for the City of Tacoma, Washington, said, "Being able to know what otherness feels like really is a gift."

Mikle McBride, a high school teacher in the Los Angeles school district, remembers being told about the Holocaust when in middle school and not understanding how "someone would be bad towards someone who was different than them." That was his first inkling that "maybe where I live is the exception, not the rule." Now, as an educator, he feels the most important lesson that he teaches is to be "open to different ideas and cultures." He believes if you can't find a physical community that is diverse, you must build the sense of community by volunteering and helping your neighbor. In 1986, the McBrides moved from Fifty-first Boulevard in Sherman Park to Shorewood. Mikle remembers a realtor talking to their new neighbors, asking if they were comfortable with the fact that the house was being sold to a black family. The McBrides received different treatment in Shorewood than they had received in Sherman Park.

Julie Jackson remembers, at the age of ten, traveling with her family when a restaurant waitress asked if Jackson would like a separate check. Now she is an accountant in Harley Davidson's personnel department and finds her "mindset of inclusion" allows her to have "good collaborative relations" at company road rallies in Asia and Europe. Her background helps her have productive relationships with everyone from the motorcycle guy with a long beard who loves bikes to the introverted guy in Asia with whom she is working on a project.

Patrick Mulvey, a reading and language arts fifth- and sixth-grade teacher at Woodland School in Milwaukee, said, "Diversity seemed normal and natural, anything else seemed abnormal." The lack of diversity "is seen as close minded and mistaken." Brian Beaudet, who teaches history at Milwaukee's High School for the Arts enjoys telling stories to his students about "just being kids" in Sherman Park. Beaudet talks to his students about having a sense of ownership in their community. He looks at his floor of the Milwaukee High School of the Arts as "Grant Boulevard." If something was not right or some students were acting up, he asks the student to "get off my floor!" He encourages the students to work and not just to take care of themselves. Beaudet controls "what happens in the classroom" and feels that every student can be successful. Others outside the immediate family can have an impact on a student, just as the adults on Grant Boulevard had an impact on him.

CHAPTER 5

BUILDING COMMUNITY

When the streetlights came on we had to go home.
—Interview by Julie Jackson

It takes a village to raise a child.
—Hillary Rodham Clinton

Neighbors watched the kids of their block, and the consequences of misbehavior could be more severe from a neighbor than one's parents. Children were welcome to scan a neighbor's refrigerator for treats and often were fed lunch. Mona Sutphen counted seventy-two kids her age in their two-block area. David Sutphen remembers the time when the neighborhood kids were playing "kick the can," and a passerby rang their doorbell and asked, "Which house is the orphanage?"

During the long summer days, children played outside from morning to dusk. There were plenty of neighborhood stores where they could spend their allowance. The bakery on North Avenue, just east of Finney Library, sold pumpkin seeds, lemon heads, jawbreakers and penny candy cherries. Al's candy store near the corner of Center and Sherman sold Ruth Nervig's favorite, Sour Patch hard candy. Homes located on high-traffic streets were good locations for Kool Aid stands and car washes.

Sidewalks were the kid's play structure. A favorite game of Tieg Whaley-Smith was to take two crushed aluminum soda cans on his front sidewalk and shoot a basketball to hit the can. Scoring was ten points for

Christmas carolers on Thirty-eighth Street. *Front:* Adrian Body and Tanya Body. *Rear:* unknown, unknown, Jackie Verser. *Courtesy of Tieg-Whaley.*

Sidewalk art on Thirty-eighth Street. *From left to right:* Alecia Davis, Haydeè Smith and Tanya Body. *Courtesy of Tieg-Whaley.*

the first struck can and twenty for the second. Of course, there was always time to have a quick, pick-up game of "kick the can." While hanging out on Sherman Boulevard, Steven Hintz would flag down police cars to get Brewer's baseball cards being given out as part of a community educational program. In 1982, the Brewers were in the series, and the cards were very popular.

The alleys were busy in summer. According to Michael Mulvey, his family had "a nice rim" in their backyard where kids from the entire neighborhood would amble down the alley and ask to join the game. He described this as an "interesting intersection," as they did not necessarily know the names of those who joined the game: "We just played basketball." Gary Glynn had to lock up his basketball hoop so his neighbors could get some sleep.

There was always something going on. Steven Hintz and his friends made a clubhouse in the attic of a neighbor's garage, complete with a coffee can for emergencies. Hintz remembers finding a man who had slept there overnight and wondering "what the hell he was doing there." Hintz and a buddy bought fireworks from a "creepy guy" who sold them out of his basement. The kids believed that the guy, who had an intercom, was "the richest person in the world!" They loved to ring the doorbell and listen to the homeowner say, "Who is it?" or "Go away!"

Finney Library, on the corner of North and Sherman Boulevard, was a mecca for kids. Ruth Nervig liked to walk over to the library during the summer and participate in the reading program. She recalls one summer reading through the entire children's book section, reading every book on the shelf. Patrick Mulvey spent so much time at the library in his early teens that his mother accused him of having a crush on Jean Straus, the librarian.

Halloween was a major holiday on Grant Boulevard and in Sherman Park. Neighbors organized a block party, blocking the street off and serving hot cider. Julie Jackson said that her Mom "went all out" for this holiday. On the day appointed by the city for trick or treating, kids from all over urban Milwaukee came because parents knew the area was friendly and safe.

The fun continued in winter. Ice-skating at the rink in Sherman Park was popular. One winter, after an especially heavy snowfall, the kids in the 2900 block of Grant Boulevard made a ten-foot slide from a garage roof. Steven Hintz, David Rogness and Brian Beaudet remember digging tunnels in the high snow banks on Locust while waiting for their school bus. They were trying to tunnel to each of their homes.

Groups of guys created their own lore. One group came up with the idea of chasing a wasp nest in a discarded couch in the alley by lighting the couch on fire. As the fire began to burn out of control, one of the boys ran to his home and got a small bowl of water to throw on the fire. That was ineffective, the flames were starting to lick the garage, so they went back in the house and got the family popcorn bowl. The kids called for help when the paint on the corner of the garage started to bubble. Their closest neighbor, a man who owned a motorcycle and dressed in a leather sleeveless vest with the look of Harley Davidson, filled an old metal garbage can with water. With a loud expletive, he dumped the water on the couch. A dad from next door brought out a very small kitchen fire extinguisher, which was ineffective given the size of the fire. The fire department arrived and quickly put out the fire. The neighbors were the first responders, although they lacked the right tools.

Another tall tale is the story of how one of the boys slid into the mouth of a large alligator in a neighbor's backyard. Recoiling in fear, the boy cried out, "It's got me, it's got me." He then noticed that there was a bullet hole in the scull of the alligator, and the guys hypothesized that the alligator had outgrown his cage and a neighbor had taken it out in the backyard and dispatched it.

There was a need for a youth service agency in Sherman Park to serve one of the city's fastest growing youth populations. In 1983, Michele Goldstein was hired by the Boys Club to start a club in the Sherman Park pavilion. "There were lots of kids and a shortage of services," explains Goldstein. She was the Milwaukee Boys' Club's first female director and recalls that she failed to understand the significance of this when she was hired. Sherman Park and the Hillside Boys Club were the only two co-ed clubs in the city, and only men ran basketball teams. The organization changed its name to the Boys and Girls Club in the late '80s.

By the end of summer 1983, the club had over one hundred members and was serving more than fifty children daily. The programming was all outdoors, so if it rained, the staff improvised activities inside the pavilion. In the morning, the tables, chairs and game equipment were rolled out of a small room once used as a room that had served a few card players. William Geenen remembers his beat-up cardboard membership card. "Lots of time it gave me something to do," Geenen said.

Goldstein moved the club to the Sherman Park Lutheran Church when winter arrived, and the club met in the basement underneath the church's roller-skating rink. The rink was a throwback to earlier years, with a sound booth, flashing lights, a turntable and a microphone. Ruth Nervig learned to roller skate here and often made up her own skating routines with a friend.

The county created a game room and an art room for the Boys and Girls Club in the basement of the Sherman Park pavilion with the support of Sherman Park's county supervisor, Paul Mathews, a resident of Sherman Park, and Dave Schultz, the director of county parks in 1985. The club rented buses to take kids to Brewer Games and Washington Park for swimming. Carla Jackson, a fifteen-year-old youth worker, ran a popular art program. The gentle summer winds carried the club's PA announcements throughout the neighborhood. It was a noisy and active place. By 1988, the club had over four hundred members and was serving over one hundred kids daily. Plans were drawn up to build a full facility, with the Boys and Girls Club covering operating costs while the county paid for the new building. The Mary Ryan Boys and Girls Club in Sherman Park was an early example of partnering between non-profit and government to help keep the parks going.

Neighborhood Enterprises

On North Avenue and Center and Burleigh Street, there were many churches, small grocery stores, restaurants, video stores, pharmacies, bars and laundries. Community Baptist Church, where Alderman Reverend Roy Neighbors was the pastor, had an ice cream social for the neighborhood every summer. St. Anne's Catholic Church started a group of block clubs, called Neighbors United, in the area around Thirty-fifth and Center. The Clear Horizon Co-op, managed by residents, and Marlene's Dance Studio, where children from the neighborhood took dance lessons, are two examples of specialty businesses in Sherman Park. The Boulevard Inn, located where the Milwaukee Public Library is today, was a neighborhood landmark. Couples enjoyed going there for special occasions.

One of the most popular bars on the Westside was the Interlude. It was where politicians and community activists hung out. The Interlude opened in 1981, was privately owned by a handful of neighborhood residents and was incorporated as a for-profit, economic development endeavor. Cooperation Westside, CAUSA, Triangle and Sherman Park, all members of the Westside Community Development Corporation

The Interlude. *Courtesy of James Baker.*

(WCDC), had submitted the application for a tax-exempt certificate. While not within Sherman Park's boundaries, "The Lude," located at the corner of Lisbon and Fortieth Street, was a gathering place for Sherman Park residents and their kids. Kids enjoyed playing the arcade games and eating nachos while the parents drank beer with their friends and discussed community issues.

Paul Henningsen, who was elected alderman of the district on the near west side in 1983, was the first president of the Interlude's board. The hope was to make a profit that could be used to purchase this and other buildings on the west side, as it was difficult to purchase real estate with money from foundations or government.

The training program at the restaurant was targeted at juveniles and adults getting out of prison who were having difficulties finding jobs. This was the justification for being certified as a non-profit business. The entrepreneurs had negotiated with the state prison system to train people as cooks, bartenders and workers for the front of the house. A ten-week training program for non-violent offenders would provide a work record that the Interlude employees would use to get a family supporting jobs. Older adults and handicapped people were hired for maintenance positions.

The nearby Harley Davidson plant provided customer traffic, and the bar was famous for its broasted chicken. The kitchen floor had to be scrubbed down three times during the first Friday night the restaurant opened because so many fish fry plates were sold. Local artists displayed their works in the restaurant, and up-and-coming music groups performed on the weekends.

Jim Gowers, a portly Texan, lived upstairs and managed the place. "The board nit-picked him to death," getting into the minutest details, Henningsen said. For example, members of the board were concerned that serving Chivas Regal did not fit into the restaurant's image as a workingman's bar even though one customer spent thirty dollars daily on this top-shelf liquor. The board had a lengthy discussion over a customer complaint about a full-figured waitress who did not wear enough underwear.

The restaurant had two large and very old pressure cookers for its signature broasted chicken. The broasters were caked with years of oil, and the board thought, "Oh my god, we have to clean that up," according to Henningsen. A few of the board members went to a car dealership on a Saturday, armed with a few beers to make the work go smoother, and cleaned both broasters with a high-pressure steam cleaner also used to clean dirty engine blocks. The broasted chicken did not taste the same after that, as something had been lost. The broasted chicken business declined.

The board became suspicious about how the money was being handled and hired a security firm to see what was going on. It turned out that the bartender was "ringing short" and taking some of the cash. The Interlude closed because the federal and state withholding taxes had not been paid. Board members ended up paying the shortfall out of their own pockets.

Other popular neighborhood events in the 1980s included "Jazz in the Park" with artists Penny Goodwin and Berkley Fudge, both recruited by Seymour Lefco, Sherman Park's jazz expert. In 1982, the Milwaukee Symphony performed a well-attended concert at the Sherman Park Lutheran Church. Bill Malone, executive director at the time, called this one of SPCA's most successful fundraisers.

In the spring of 1986, Paul Mathews and Mike Brodd launched the Sherman Park Yacht Club, a tongue-in-cheek promotion that was in direct response to "the very real threat of erosion resulting in the relocation of Bradford Beach to somewhere just west of Twenty-seventh Street,"

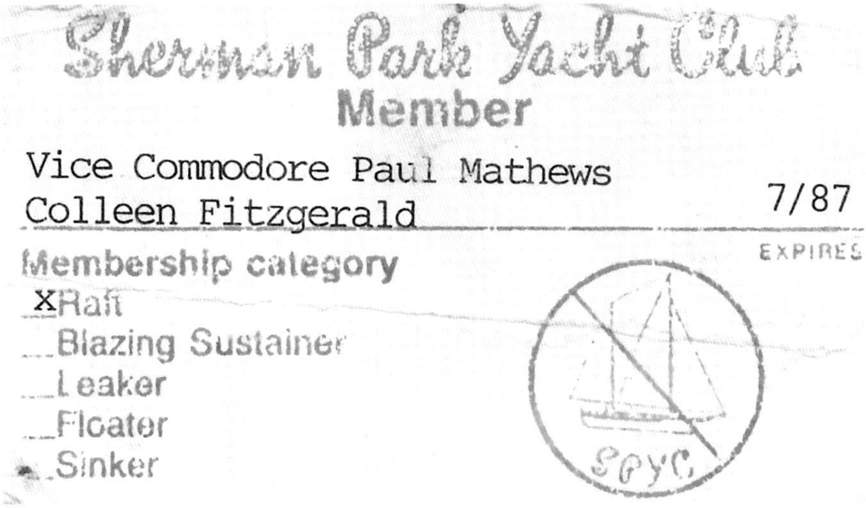
Sherman Park Yacht Club
Member
Vice Commodore Paul Mathews
Colleen Fitzgerald 7/87
EXPIRES
Membership category
x Raft
__Blazing Sustainer
__Leaker
__Floater
__Sinker
SPYC

Official membership card for Sherman Park Yacht Club. *Courtesy of Paul Mathews.*

according to Commodore Brodd. The concept was developed over a couple of beers one evening while the two were reading a yachting book. At the time, the Lake Michigan water level was at a historic high, and the bluffs overlooking the lake were experiencing heavy erosion. This became a "really fun way of promoting our neighborhood," Mathews said. The event was launched with a press event at Washington Park, where an entire truckload of sand was dumped in the parking lot as a visual aid. Local Milwaukee sun worshiper Dick Bacon added his support to the group at the press conference.

In June, the first SPYC paddleboat regatta was held on Lake Dineen, complete with a "Yats of Brats" cookout following the race. Unfortunately, there is no record of which boat won the heavily competed for and much coveted trophy. Late in October 1986, more than one hundred SPYC members, decked out in their nautical caps, paraded around the city, proudly displaying their membership plaques hanging around their necks. SPYC sponsored other events, such as a special fundraising concert by Walter and the White Guys at Capital Court and the Yats of Voices Christmas caroling group that entertained neighborhood residents.

A Community Within a Community

The Orthodox Jewish community in the area around Fifty-first Boulevard and Burleigh was seeing growth. Among those moving in were Howard Karsh and his family who moved in 1973 from Glendale to Sherman Park to join Rabbi Michael Twerski's Beth Jehudah Synagogue. The Borsuk family moved to Sherman Park ten years after the Karshes. Alan Borsuk, a reporter for the *Milwaukee Journal* on the city desk, was writing his annual summer article for the Sunday magazine. A friend who lived on Fifty-first Boulevard suggested that Borusk interview Rabbi Michel Twerski and his wife, Feige, about their Orthodox congregation. Borsuk's interview of Rabbi Twerski grew into an invitation to spend the Sabbath with the Twerskis. A deep friendship developed, and the Borsuks joined the Orthodox Community, purchasing a home near Beth Jehudah in 1983.

In the early 1980s, many of the Jewish children in the Sherman Park community were attending Hillel Academy in White Fish Bay. Hillel Academy's Reform curriculum was "not quite what they were looking for," according to Borsuk, and Rabbi Twerski decided that the Orthodox Jewish community needed its own school. The members of the synagogue wanted an institution that would prepare their children for an education in a yeshiva high school and college. In 1989, Yeshiva Elementary School, a kindergarten through eighth-grade school with sixty-four students, opened at 3447 North Fifty-first, with Karsh as the school's first administrator. To meet the adult education needs of the members of the congregation, Milwaukee Kollel, an institute that offers extensive lectures and classes to adults on a wide range of Jewish topics, was opened the same year. It had six rabbis teaching post-graduate studies during the day and adult education classes in the evening.

Funding was never easy, especially at the start. The Jewish Federation of North America, a national organization, saw Yeshiva Elementary School as a competitor to Hillel Academy and refused to fund the new schools. Rabbi Twerski and Karsh went on a national fundraising tour, asking people to come to their rescue even though synagogues had their own schools to support. Rabbi Twerski was the chief fundraiser for Yeshiva Elementary until new funding sources became available through Partners Advancing Values in Education (PAVE), an organization that funds private schools, and School Choice Wisconsin, the state funding program for private schools.

Yeshiva Elementary School was to help its students and their families better understand what it meant to be an Orthodox Jew. Young families started moving to Sherman Park to become part of this community. People purchased homes and apartments so that they could walk to Beth Jehudah on the Sabbath. In the late 1990s, the Linda Daniel Bader Foundation funded a seven-year program to grow the Orthodox community in Sherman Park. Karsh was executive director of this outreach program that advertised throughout the country for families, offering help with mortgages, home repair and jobs. Yeshiva Elementary School, as the only kindergarten through eighth grade Orthodox Jewish school in the entire country, and Milwaukee Kollel Institute, with its resources to teach Jewish literacy, became a draw for families looking to join an Orthodox synagogue.

Members of Beth Jehudah "live within the Sherman Park community with a level of separateness," as Karsh explains it. Members live in the world on a journey driven by faith. Their children do not have the same privileges and freedoms that other kids have. They can't eat food prepared by someone outside of their community. Participating in block parties on Saturdays are not possible.

Borsuk, who restricts his volunteer activities due to being the Education reporter with the *Milwaukee Journal Sentinel*, describes the Jewish community relationship with SPCA as being fairly low-key. Echoing Karsh's comments, Borsuk said, "The traditional Jewish lifestyle is pretty involving and time consuming, with the institutions that they created taking up a huge amount of time and energy." What members of this community do for fun is entirely different than what their non-Jewish neighbors do. Orthodox Jews do not have televisions, for one.

The influx of Jewish people into an area between Burleigh and Keefe and Forty-ninth to Fifty-sixth also resulted in non-Jewish people staying, stabilizing the area. This "just happened. It was not planned," Karsh said. By 2012, 180 Jewish families (165 of them in their own homes) and a thousand family members lived in the area. Borsuk feels that this community is still "a fragile franchise," though it is "much more energized than it was in 1983 when they moved in." The Borsuks' neighbors, Larry and Nancy Siewert, were close friends. The Siewert's daughter, Mikaala, is the same age as their second-oldest daughter, and the two families have always been close. Larry Siewert handled small household emergencies on the Sabbath, and the Siewerts' older children babysat for the Borsuks. This is a good snapshot of religious diversity in Sherman Park as Siewert, a Roman Catholic, formerly a principal of Marquette High School, was one of the founders of a Catholic middle school on the south side of Milwaukee.

The Beth Jehudah Synagogue is a village within a neighborhood within a mid-sized city where residents watch their kids walk to their neighborhood school. Multiple generations of families either live together or have plans to return when their education is completed. There is a deep sense of belonging that goes beyond what words can describe.

Camelot

The next generation learned important lessons while growing up in Sherman Park, and sometimes view it as a special place and one that is impossible to recreate. They remember it as a golden time when the world was perfect and safe. The hard work of building community is not always recalled.

CHAPTER 6

CHALLENGES IN THE '80S

At first it seemed that it was growing, they built those houses on the freeway, then things started to decay, houses went into default. That initial growth did not turn into anything.
—Steven Hintz

In the 1980s, new issues arose to threaten the quality of life in Sherman Park, replacing the former focus on housing discrimination, the freeway and desegregating the schools. Plans for light rail down Sherman Boulevard and crime were new issues that threatened the neighborhood. In addition, SPCA and SPRC were experiencing communication problems with their members, committees and boards as they struggled to deal with an expanded staff.

CRIME

In 1982, President Regan declared the War On Drugs, a label that moved drug use from a private matter with public-health ramifications to a threat to the well being of the entire nation. Nationally, drug use, including cocaine, rose dramatically between 1983 and 1985 and then started to rapidly decline, leveling off in 1992, according to Devah Pager in *Marked.* Surveys in 1988 of city of Milwaukee residents show that most residents saw crime on the rise, but their perception did not match actual crime statistics. Violent and property crimes leveled off in the 1980s and then fell by 30 percent during 1990s. The only exception to this was the bump in drug related crimes in the mid-1980s.

The perception of the time that the world was more dangerous was fed by media accounts. A network news study covering the period of 1990 to 1997 documented the fact that crime news stories were featured more than any other subject, including the economy and health care, according to Pager in *Marked*. Another study of network news programs of the period between 1990 and 1991 found that "a predictable 'us against them' frame was used in the news stories, with 'us' being white, suburban America, and 'them' being black Americans," according to Michelle Alexander in *The New Jim Crow*.

There is anecdotal evidence about the rise in property, violent and drug crime in Sherman in the mid-1980s. A 1986 *Milwaukee Journal* article cited the fact that Sherman Park had the second highest number of property crimes the prior year. Residents were experiencing break-ins and robberies. Alderman Tom Donegan's home was broken into five times. Chris McAuliffe's new home in Park Renaissance on the developed freeway land was broken into three times. Jeff McCreary remembers residents being attacked walking from their garages to their homes.

Children of Sherman Park experienced crime on a personal level. Robberies and physical violence were part of their childhood. Ruth Nervig said, "I never felt particularly safe in Sherman Park. I distinctly remember roller skating…when I was about seven years old and a man passed us with a gun in his back pocket." Steven Hintz remembered, "We were increasingly getting our stuff stolen." Hintz and David Rogness had their tennis racquets stolen on the way to play tennis in Sherman Park. Two of the Mulvey brothers had their breakfast cereal stolen on their walk home from the Super American convenience store on North Avenue. Brian Beaudet's home was broken into, and the thieves took everything, trashing the house. Julie Jackson remembers finding their home burglarized and the back door off its hinges. Karl Pearson-Cater said that when he was ten or eleven, he could leave his bike outside, but by the time he was eighteen, he had to be careful. Pearson-Cater was attacked twice in Sherman Park.

Cory Thompson was robbed at knifepoint walking home from the library. A bus pulled up, and a passenger, his arms filled with a large bag of groceries, chased the assailants off. Thompson, shaken, ran to James and Mary Walrath's home, where the police were called. Michael Mulvey

Thirty-eighth Street neighbors get together to clean off a recent graffiti attack (1982). *Courtesy of Tieg Whaley-Smith.*

Boarded up, foreclosed homes affect surrounding home values. Thirty-eighth Street promoted this home so it could be sold before it became the victim of vandals (1982). *Courtesy of Tieg Whaley-Smith.*

was surrounded by a gang of youths and knocked to the ground as he was meeting his friends at the baseball diamond in Sherman Park.

Kids learned how to deal with verbal harassment on the city buses. Sarah Geenen was bullied, and Sarah's friend was pushed off the bus, her sister Kristin remembers. Bus riders sometimes would attempt to steal the sisters' shoes or pop them on the back of their heads, Sarah Geenen said. The young adults would make a plan on how they were going to handle the nasty kids on the bus. "What was weird, we never told [our parents] about this," Sarah said.

Sarah remembers when she and her sister Kristin Powers saw a women being physically assaulted on the bus by her male companion. The sisters and their friends, questioning why the bus driver did not get involved, followed the couple and threatened the assailant with rocks. "We felt so comfortable. We had this model that if something is wrong, we should do something about it," Geenen said.

Kristin remembers finding a baggie filled with white powder in their backyard. Geenen related that her bike was stolen while they were visiting a neighbor. Patricia Geenen, the girls' mother, found Sarah's stolen bike by driving through the alleys. Sarah remembers being "more scared at what Mom was going to do" than whether they would get her bike back.

A violent sexual assault of Patricia Geenen while she was taking her daily walk in Washington Park galvanized the neighborhood. Everyone gathered around to help, meals showed up on the family's doorstep and a Lutheran minister stood outside her window at St. Anthony's hospital window and prayed. Patricia Geenen was a tough woman. Returning home after a short stay at the hospital, although still feeling violated, she interacted with a steady stream of friends and neighbors. Everyone wanted to be assured that she would be OK. Several weeks later, she joined her neighbors in a march against violence to the pavilion at Washington Park. The march was effective. The Milwaukee County Sheriff's Department set up a small office in Washington Park.

Geenen's assault in Washington Park was a strong memory for the children of Sherman Park. Sarah Geenen said that she thought Sherman Park was a safe community until her mom got hurt. Her sister, Kristin, said in an interview, "Definitely, one of my strongest memories was when my Mom was attacked and the march through the park." Steven Hintz remembers this assault as something that "he was pretty scared about." Brian Beaudet recalled that the *Milwaukee Journal* ran a photo of some of his friends marching to Washington Park. Some people put in security systems, and others moved. Brian Beaudet said that his friends moving seemed "like sticks being scattered in the wind."

Burnout

No community can continue that level of energy…and it is absolutely unbelievable that they did this for as long as they did.
—Jerome Brandl

Between 1977 and 1984, Sherman Park Community Association had eight executive directors, half of them cycling through on short terms near the end of this period. Financial controls were loose, cash flow was problematic and the United Way funding was spent by mid-year, forcing the layoff of staff. Bob Nicol said that on his first day as executive director, the staff consisted of himself and the receptionist, as the rest had quit because of the termination of the former executive director.

In 1983, a non-profit management consulting organization interviewed the committees, board and staff and issued a report that cited a "loss of direction, a lack of priorities, poor communication, confusion as the roles of board and staff over policy-setting, lack of volunteers, drop in membership and fund raising, and lack of representation on the board," according to Juliet Saltman in *A Fragile Movement*.

Managing SPCA was a difficult job. Some of SPCA's executive directors weighed in on this issue in their UWM Oral History interviews. Greta Hansen said, "People think the organization can do it all on its own once it has staff." William Malone accused two committees of operating "autonomously," using the SPCA name and resources but operating outside the control of the board of directors and staff. Corinne Cahill felt that the fifteen-member SPCA board had a difficult time communicating with the organization's numerous committees. Robert Nicol felt that attending all of the evening committee meetings "was an impossible task."

Burnout was always a problem. Carol Holton, one of SPCA's early presidents, said in an interview that SPCA "was an impossible organization to work for." SPCA's mission was so broad, and implementing that mission demanded so much time by staff and volunteers, that executive director Robert Nicol mused, "I don't know how anyone can hold that job for any length of time."

Recruiting new board members and keeping dedicated members involved was an ongoing problem. Serving on working committees involved lots of tension, and having them coordinate with the board was difficult. Keeping track of issues the committees and the board were working on was "almost impossible," according to Nicol. The issues had shifted from brick-and-mortar projects to more complex ones that did not have such visible signs of "victory," according to William Malone, one of SPCA's executive directors.

The board had difficulties in recruiting and keeping new board members, and many were inexperienced in the art of fundraising. Procedures for evaluating the performance of staff had to be developed. The executive director was in a constant fundraising mode, leaving little time for personnel and board issues. The goals were longer range for the whiter and better-off western section of Sherman Park than those who lived in the lower-income eastern section, which had more immediate issues, thought William Malone, one of SPCA's executive directors.

Over forty block clubs were organized in one summer to give residents a voice. St. Joseph's Hospital provided seed money for the program that had six volunteers equipped with two-way radios, drawn from a pool of six hundred residents, driving around the neighborhood from dusk to 10:30 p.m. Over time, participation in the Neighborhood Watch Program declined because of the huge amount of volunteer resources required.

Light Rail

In 1980, the Sherman Park neighborhood opposed a planned light-rail line routed down the median of Sherman Boulevard. It was felt that this would divide the community, isolating the eastern section from the western section. People might feel that they lived on the "wrong side of the tracks."

Ridership projections were not credible to Sherman Park residents. The African American community opposed a route down Fond du Lac Avenue, and the route down the Thirtieth Street rail corridor was promoted as the best alternative to these other two routes. Route 30 of the Milwaukee County transit system, which ran on Sherman Boulevard, had the highest ridership of any route in the system. Light rail would build on that success. But the South East Regional Planning Commission would not use the high ridership of Route 30 for the Thirtieth Street Rail Corridor, eliminating the old rail right-of-way completely. Sherman Boulevard was "a treasured asset," and "the character of the street" would be "destroyed," according to Nicol, the executive director of SPCA. Signs opposing light rail lined Sherman Boulevard from Capital Court to Washington Park.

Former mayor John Norquist said, "Opposition by Sherman Park to light rail might have been a mistake. If it had been built, it would have made the neighborhood healthy." He feels that middle-class homeowners would have been attracted by the convenience of light rail, along with the beautiful architecture and the craftsmen-built homes. Bill Drew thought the plan was tossed out because "people did not understand what was happening." Mayor Tom Barrett, Milwaukee's mayor today, pointed out that light rail had not yet become "an ideological war." This may have been a missed opportunity, as based on today's knowledge, it would have not been the racial dividing line of the neighborhood.

Redevelopment of the Park West Freeway Land

Congressman Henry Reuss established the Park West Redevelopment Task Force and appointed David Hoeh as chairperson. Mayor Henry Maier felt strongly that the development of the freeway land was his responsibility and did not allow staff from the city's Department of City Development to work with the Park West Task Force.

In fall of 1983, Chris and Mac McAuliffe moved into one of the first houses built in the Park Renaissance development on the cleared freeway land. Their neighbors were "a wonderful mix of people who had chosen to be pioneers," Chris McAuliffe said. They were racially and economically diverse, in the Sherman Park tradition, and had made a conscious decision to live here. Finney Library, located nearby on North Avenue, was vibrant and heavily used. The McGuire's organized block parties, published a local resident directory and signed neighborhood kids up for soccer. They were really excited about living there and wanted to make sure all the new homes were sold.

Problems with the quality of the houses in the entire neighborhood surfaced after three years, and although complaints were lodged with the builders, the Sampsons, it was difficult to get the issues resolved. In October 1987, the McAuliffes lost both their jobs on the same day. Since their home was "under water," it went into foreclosure and the couple moved out in spring of 1988.

Residents look over plans developed by the Parkwest Redevelopment Task Force for the freeway land (1982). *Milwaukee Public Library Humanities Dept Park West Freeway.*

DIFFICULT ECONOMIC TIMES

Tieg Whaley-Smith remembers his father taking him to see thousands of people lined up at A.O. Smith to fill out job applications. His father told him that this was a visible sign of the lack of jobs in Milwaukee. In 1980, the median family income in the Sherman Park area was $17,000, slightly higher than the entire city's median income of $16,060. The median income in the eastern section was $13,500, while the central and western sections' median incomes were $20,800 and $20,000 respectively, according to Juliet Saltman in *A Fragile Movement.* By 1985, 40 percent of Sherman

Katie Doyle organized a Not For Sale event to promote Sherman Park as a good place to live. The photo was taken on the 2400 block of North Forty-seventh Street around 1988. *Courtesy of Jim Wend.*

The Hughs children, the Wends' neighbors on the 2400 block of North Forty-seventh (1988). *Courtesy of Jim Wend.*

Park's population consisted of minorities, and the population had dropped by almost 8 percent. Sherman Park residents lost over three thousand jobs between 1979 and 1985.

People stayed through these difficult economic times. Longtime resident Nancy Spransey said she "still likes her neighbors" and that she has a strong feeling of community. Bradley Hausler purchased his home from the Sherman Park Redevelopment Corporation in the eastern section of Sherman Park in 1987 and continues to live there today. He loves the quality of his home and the convenience of where he lives. Hausler describes himself as one of the few "stalwarts" that owns his home on a block with a preponderance of rentals. He said being the only white person on a whole block was not as fearful as he thought once people got to know him.

CHAPTER 7

THE NEXT GENERATION

They developed into someone who can go out in the world and do something.
—Elaine Stalheim

Social Capital

Robert Putnam, in *Bowling Alone,* said people in a community working together increase productivity in the same manner a tool increases physical capital or an education increases human capital. Putnam called this "social capital." The kids that grew up in Sherman Park demonstrate the impact of diversity in the careers they chose and the families they are raising. "You learn to not take people at face value, you see no bar to having friends, it is just a natural part of our lives," Mona Sutphen said. The diversity in Sherman Park and the social capital it creates "does not surprise me, since you see segregation more outside the city than within the city," Milwaukee's Mayor Tom Barrett said. Strong communication skills, one attribute of social capital, can be seen in the next generation of Sherman Park.

The next generation made important connections in college while their classmates were learning how to interact with other races. They made friends and met future spouses that positioned them to earn wide-ranging positions from the White House staff to teaching history in a Milwaukee high school. These are bridge people with a broad view of the world who

Kids with large ball (1982). *Courtesy of Tieg Whaley-Smith.*

don't see themselves as black or white but are proud of their entire racial heritage and traditions.

The benefits of diversity were passed on to the next generation. An article written by *Milwaukee Journal* reporter Jason Abul Alim impressed Elaine Stalheim, former principal of Thirty-eighth School, and she responded with an affirming email. Alim wrote her back that he was a former student at Thirty-eighth Grade School, then known as Jason Bonert. Alim had enjoyed reading his compositions to Stalheim in her principal's office. Stalheim commented how the success of her students was across racial lines, citing Jason Bonert, Tieg Whaley and Amon as examples. Paul Mathews observed that his generation was "really struggling with diversity," but the next generation is much more open and accepting," a gift that "we were able to pass on to them."

Sutphen observed that often people's understanding "of other communities was limited." Her experiences growing up in Sherman Park resulted in her own family having a diverse group of friends, and they are "really engaged" with different races and religions and with their community. Living in New York City, their children see a diverse community as a normal condition.

Sutphen believes that their young children will be just as interested in politics and engaged in their community as they are. "They will pick that up naturally," Sutphen said.

Sutphen was White House Deputy Chief of Staff for Policy for President Obama for two years, from January 2009 to January 2011. Today she is managing director at UBS AG, covering geopolitical risk, macro-policy trends and their impact on the global economy. She is considered to be an expert in national and world economic issues and is the co-author of the book *The Next Century: How the U.S. Can Thrive as Other Powers Rise.*

David Sutphen, Mona's brother, said, "It has been quite notable how many people from this neighborhood have been involved in the present administration [of President Obama], working to make the world a better place from the progressive viewpoint." One of David Sutphen's best friends in college was Harold Ford. In November 1996, Ford was elected to fill his father's seat in Congress. Sutphen left the law firm he was working for and became Ford's Chief of Staff. Today Sutphen is managing partner of the Washington, D.C. office of Brunswick Group, an international corporate communications consulting company that specializes in technology and media.

David said that his parents were deliberate in exposing him to an environment where "everyone grew to appreciate diversity." He feels that when they do have children, it will be important for them to live in the same "multi dimensional environment" world. He wants his kids to have the same experiences so they can "navigate our multiethnic society."

Jonathan McBride, deputy assistant to the president, works in a busy, crowded office in the large Eisenhower Office Building adjacent to the White House. Before joining the White House staff, McBride was the co-founder of a publishing company for young professionals called Jungle Media Group. He is part of the team that is responsible for recruiting and keeping management talent for President Obama's administration.

He first realized as a college student, "when he got out of the bubble," that he had a "distinctively different" experience in Sherman Park. His parents had been encouraging him to be politically active, even as a young boy, taking him along when canvassing and having him help with mailings and literature drops.

"You don't walk into a neighborhood like Sherman Park. You build it! It's a commitment that you make" McBride said in an article by Jim Stingle published in the *Milwaukee Journal* in 2006. McBride wrote later, "Many of us are looking for neighborhoods that offer our families a diverse environment in which to grow. People should have the optimism that they too can create neighborhoods like this."

McBride's job as deputy director of presidential personnel in President Barack Obama's administration is to recruit "positive diversity around the table and bring as many perspectives around the problem as you can." This is a major premise behind President Obama's philosophy of innovation in his administration, McBride explains. You need "a lot of perspectives when you are dealing with a problem of national or world scale."

McBride recruits people for President Obama's administration who are able to "draw out the diversity that is around the table," empowering different communication styles and skills. When talking to White House groups, McBride uses the story of Sherman Park's resistance to a new freeway as an organizing platform. He feels that Sherman Park is a model for the entire country.

Mikle McBride uses Sherman Park in his U.S. History class at Hawthorne High School in Los Angeles. As an educator, he tries to teach his students to treat people with respect and be open to different ideas and cultures. He has not found a physical community like Sherman Park but is still part of a community, "doing volunteer stuff." McBride said in an interview, "Today in Los Angeles, neighborhoods that are racially and economically integrated are very rare." He said a community is "not just about you. You help your neighbors out. You talk to them!" Being able to "navigate myself through different populations served me well when I got to college and it still serves me well."

Patrick Mulvey teaches Reading and Language Arts to fifth and sixth graders at Woodland School, a charter grade school in Milwaukee. Woodland School started many years ago as the Alverno Campus elementary school, where some Sherman Park parents sent their children in the '70s and '80s. Mulvey feels that the days one can have the same experience that he did are gone, but he sees Woodland School providing the same sense of community for his children that Sherman Park did. He made a decision to place his children at Woodland School as he wanted them to grow up thinking that "diversity is the norm." Mulvey describes the school as a diverse, functioning community. The lack of diversity is "close minded," and he wants his children to be in a "connected community."

Michael Mulvey is a high school math teacher at Nathan Hale High School in West Allis after teaching in two Milwaukee Public School high schools. He tries to be aware of both race and class and credits his sensitivity to his experiences growing up in Sherman Park. Michael sees the incident of his assault in Sherman Park by gang members as something he wants to "insulate his kids from." Kathy Mulvey, mother of Patrick and Michael, commented that their oldest and youngest sons, both teachers, bring their experiences growing up in Sherman Park to their careers as teachers.

Corey Thompson is chairperson of the Urban Education Program at Cardinal Stritch University in Milwaukee. One of his messages for new teachers placed in urban schools, such as Milwaukee public schools, is training teachers to become "intentional advocates" for their students, and he credits Sherman Park as an "example of intentional diversity."

Thompson and his wife, Kiki, were members of Elmbrook Church in Brookfield while they lived in Menominee Falls, Wisconsin. It was a convenient location, being about twenty minutes away from both sets of parents. This was not the diversity that they were looking for, and the family moved to Sherman Park, joining a group of twenty families that belong to the sister church, Eastbrook Church. Their new community, with people who share their faith and belief in the bible, reminds them of living on Grant Boulevard. The Thompson know all of their neighbors and their four children attend Milwaukee Public Schools. Their children experience diversity daily. They "could not be more happy with their choice," with the "revolving door of kids" coming through their home and an uncle and a grandfather living nearby.

Tieg Whaley-Smith attended Juneau High School, where he became interested in a career in business. He wanted to work to "bring jobs to the neighborhood," so after graduation he attended the University of Wisconsin–Madison, where the Afro-American studies and political science courses helped him better understand the problems in the African American community. He went to law school at the University of Michigan, specializing in community economic development, to gain the skills to solve these problems.

He started his own law practice in Milwaukee, specializing in working with non-profits building affordable housing and community revitalization projects. Between 1995 and 2012, his firm has generated 250 housing units with a total value of $50 million, 50 percent minority owned in projects, with 15 percent of the construction workers coming from the immediate neighborhood.

His family lives on Grant Boulevard, which today has African American, white and interracial families living together. He and his wife, Lindsey, who purchased their home from the Jacksons, are proud to carry on the former owners' long tradition of community involvement. The Whaley-Smith children go to MPS's McDowell Montessori School. The Whaley-Smiths see the fact that young families are moving back to Grant Boulevard as an encouraging sign.

ONE FAMILY

Success can be measured in different ways. Some members of the next generation completed college while others struggled with disabilities. One Sherman Park family is an example of how each member used skills learned in growing up there to leverage success.

Sarah Geenen is a research professor in the Regional Research Institute for Human Services at Portland State University. She provides support and services to youths who age out of traditional foster care services. Her "My Life" program helps youth set and attain early adulthood goals, such as finding an apartment or applying for college. "Even if the goal is unrealistic, we can still use it to teach skills," Geenen said. "They can still learn to break down their goals into steps, prioritize activities, learn to ask for help, build confidence as they move toward their goal." The youth also participate in quarterly workshops where they discuss topics such as interviewing for a job and finding housing, skills that those aging out of the foster care system have to learn.

Geenen's "Better Futures" program serves foster youth, with a history of mental health problems. Peer mentors who have been in foster care in the past, some of whom have struggled with homelessness and mental health issues but still have gone on to college, work with young adults in foster care. The outcomes of both of these programs have been documented in "rigorous randomized trial, and the results are impressive," says Michael Garringer, from the National Mentoring Center, in *Reflections from the 2011 Summer Institute on Youth Mentoring.* Roger Jarjoura, associate professor in the School of Public and Environmental Affairs at Indian University–Perdue University. Garringer, who is director of a mentoring program targeting juveniles in the correctional system, called this "transformative mentoring, where mentors really do change how youth think about their future and their ability to achieve."

Geenen said that her work with foster care is driven by her sense that she has the responsibility to help others who "have absolutely no political voice, no parental advocacy, no one standing up for them to make sure they get

First day of school for the Geenen family (1976). William, Michael, Kristin and Sarah. *Courtesy of Paul Geenen.*

their fair share of resources and opportunities. I came from a place where I am aware that these kind of barriers exist."

Geenen's family lives in Portland, Oregon, in a neighborhood where the definition of diversity includes sexual orientation. They actively seek out racial diversity, and their oldest son, Shanti Dubey, selected Portland's diverse Grant School High School, whose student population is equally split between minorities and white, over a private high school with great facilities and a strong soccer program. Geenen says that diversity, "in terms of who I married, his Indian background, honors the fact that there is more than one way to look at the world."

The research of Kristin Powers, professor of Advanced Studies in Education and Counseling at California State Long Beach, focuses on service delivery models in special education, school psychology services and gender equity. She has traveled to Vietnam to bring school psychology trends to professionals in the developing country.

Powers tables, marches and has spoken for the Coalition against Militarism in Schools, Legal Aid and the Long Beach Housing Authority. She is actively involved in working to improve the lives of others, and she works to build a sense of community by organizing her community's annual block party and getting everyone out for a kickball game at Christmas. Powers stays in contact with many of her Sherman Park friends, maintaining that connection even though they are spread throughout the country.

Michael Geenen and his wife, Staci, have built a strong community at Northtown Church in Milwaukee. "The people are really nice, very warm and friendly, very loving," Geenen said. Members take Michael and Staci grocery shopping weekly, and others help them budget their money. On Fifth Sunday, Michael and Staci enjoy the congregation's potluck. Staci enjoys participating in women's events, and Michael helps the guys on church maintenance projects. Recently, friends from church moved Michael and Staci to their new apartment in Milwaukee's Westlawn Housing Development.

William Geenen is a graduate of Chris Cole School for the Blind and is now a sophomore at Austin Community College, in Austin, Texas. He accepts diversity as part of his everyday life. As a member of the Student Government Association, he deals with people from many different backgrounds. Growing up in Sherman Park has enabled him to work with people of many cultural backgrounds, including the Iraqi students on campus. He sees diversity as "a good thing."

BUILDING "THE INTENTIONALITY OF COMMUNITY"

In the 2000 U.S. Census, seven million Americans declared themselves as multiracial, making this one of the fastest-growing demographics in the country, according to Nicholas Jones, chief of the U.S. Census Bureau's Racial Statistics Branch. This group is primarily from the birth of children of interracial parents.

Cory Thompson, David Sutphen and Brian Beaudet use the description of "intentionality of community" in describing the environment they seek. The next generation looks for diverse communities to raise their own children, similar to the one they were raised in. Minority births now outnumber white births in our country. By 2042, minorities will be in the majority, and this will grow to 54 percent of our country's population by 2050, according to a CNN U.S. 2008 report.

David Rogness, who is a project manager for a company that provides software for school districts, lives in McKinney, Texas, twenty minutes north of Dallas, and as he settles in to this community, it is starting to "come close to the one in Sherman Park." The parents from Sherman Park who "took me under their wing" is one feature that he would like his children to experience.

Chris McCreary attributes his attendance at specialty schools to getting to know people from "outside his community." His son, Cole, eighteen, recently graduated from Milwaukee Public School Rufus King High School, recently ranked as one of the best high schools in the state, and has applied to a number of colleges here in the United States and Canada to pursue a degree in Economics and International Business. McCreary said that his son "benefited from his Rufus King experience and got a taste of a better world."

Alan Borsuk described his four children's experiences at Yesiva Elementary as "being a small town in a big city. It offered a real lot of positiveness. The school was a very centralizing institution socially, my children are still close to the same kids that they started with in kindergarten." Two of his daughters and their families live blocks away, and his two sons attend a yeshiva in New York. Borsuk said his entire family is "quite invested in the neighborhood."

The next generation was able to put crime, which the kids all experienced, in proper perspective, understanding that it "does not make a neighborhood bad," according to James Gramling. Growing up in Sherman Park taught practical coping skills that enabled the next generation to flourish in an increasingly diverse world.

Their success is the hallmark of the diversity of Sherman Park. Success is measured both economically and socially. They might work in powerful political or corporate offices, manage a class of high school students, or cope with their physical and mental disabilities, but all create vibrant, supportive communities.

The next generation, which leveraged the social capital from the Sherman Park community and flourished, now wants the same for their children. Putman said, "Social capital matters because our networks, if they are extensive enough, connect us to potential economic partners who provide high-quality information, and vouch for us." Connections this generation made put them on the path of economic success, ranging from leadership positions in political organizations or corporations; to researchers and teachers in grade schools, high schools and higher education; to finding people who help them cope and, as Putman said, "to mitigate the insidious effects of socioeconomic disadvantage."

Building "new Sherman Parks" would also benefit our entire country. Putman said, "Given that social capital can benefit individuals, it is perhaps no surprise that it can help neighborhoods, and even entire nations, to create wealth." Diversity builds social capital as it enhances connections. Putman describes these networks as ones that connect people to "potential economic partners," who provide "high-quality information and support each other."

CHAPTER 8

CONCLUSION

Members of the next generation look for a neighborhood like Sherman Park for their families. Jonathan McBride said, "The reality is that you have to commit to building it, as you are not going to find it." The members of Sherman Park fought a ten-year fight against the freeways, overcoming the fact that 52 percent of Milwaukee County voters approved the construction of the freeways, before the Park West Freeway was demapped. The block parties, soccer and the Interlude built community and provided the tremendous amount of energy required to win this lengthy fight. Current Milwaukee mayor Tom Barrett said that the Sherman Park community is "frankly engaged more than any other community. This gives them a louder voice, allows them to address their problems more quickly and makes the neighborhood and city stronger."

President Barack Obama was a community organizer and applied those principals in structuring his reelection campaign in 2012. His autobiography, *Dreams from My Father*, written when he was in his early '30s, talks about the importance of building community. He writes, "What I needed was a community…that cut deeper than the common despair that black friends and I shared when reading the latest crime statistics, or the high fives I might exchange on a basketball court. A place where I could put down stakes and test my commitment."

Obama chose his friends carefully while he was in college, selecting those that were "more politically active," foreign students, Chicanos, feminists and poets. One of his friends he described in his book, Joyce, described herself:

"I'm *multiracial.*" Her father "*happened* to be Italian and was the sweetest man in the world; and her mother, who *happened* to be part African and part French and part American and part something else." The next generation sees their friends as individuals, irrespective of their racial heritage, avoiding stereotypes and exemplifying a model that outperforms others.

Scott Page in *The Difference* writes that diverse groups of people "outperform collections of people who rely on homogeneous perspectives." He said, "We should recognize that a talented 'I' and a talented 'they' can become an even more talented 'we.'" Page defines diversity as not just "race, gender and ethnicity," but also includes "the friendships, road trips, chance meetings, and pancake breakfasts that combine to form a life. Education and training also influence our collections of cognitive tools. Diversity has many causes." Intersecting diversity with community leverages natural ability. Scott explains, "Ability is a property of an individual—a nice shiny apple. Neither a person or an apple can be diverse. Diversity is a property of a collection of people—a basket with many kinds of fruit. The better the individual fruit, the better the fruit basket, and the better the other fruit, the better the apple." Those valuing diversity are open to exploring solutions from a wide variety of sources.

People wishing to create a diverse neighborhood similar to Sherman Park do it by making an intentional decision to raise their families in a diverse environment. This intentionality is empowering. The freeways, segregated schools and racial steering by the housing industry were the problems faced in Sherman Park in the '70s and the '80s. Today's problems include immigration, good schools and the availability of family-supporting jobs. These problems are more apt to be solved by a large, diverse group of people, according to Page. He calls for four conditions present in order for diversity to be more powerful than ability: the problem must be difficult, the "thinking tools" and perspectives of those working on solving the problems must be very diverse, the problems must be large and the number of people solving the problems must be numerous. He said that problems are solved in this environment by the exchange of "ideas, proposals, and solutions" between a community with "diverse cognitive skills."

One detects in interviews of the next generation a confidence, a worldview that seeks common ground and an ability to have, as Julie Jackson describes, "A simple conversation and good relationships with different kinds of people." Ruth Nervig feels "a sense of unity despite outer differences with people that has given me the ability to adapt to different cultures easily." Sarah Geenen said, "What constitutes a family today has changed, and we have to be more

Ball players. *Courtesy of Jim Wend.*

Three girls. *Courtesy of Jim Wend.*

active in seeking that out." The next generation shows us how to meet Page's description of a large group that effectively addresses problems.

Intentional diversity comes with risk. Growing up in Sherman Park, the next generation suffered threats, some of them physical. Today, as parents, the next generation often lives in diverse neighborhoods and sends their children to similarly diverse schools. Their children, some now in their early teens, see diversity as normal. The grandchildren of Sherman Park residents are not any more aware of their parent's intentionality than their parents were. They handle racial discrimination with aplomb and easily make friends across wide racial lines.

Jonathon McBride said, "Sherman Park is the direction the country should go, given the idealistic nature of the United States." The urban environment more easily provides a large collection of diverse and capable people. The next generation values putting their children in schools where diversity is the norm and works hard to support the school their children attend. Living in the city, sending your children to schools with diverse student bodies, being involved in politics and advocating for change—these are the hallmarks of a diverse, supportive community. It is not a place but a lifestyle. The success of the next generation from Sherman Park is evidence that diversity works.

BIBLIOGRAPHY

Alexander, Michelle. *The New Jim Crow: Mass Incarceration in the Age of Colorblindness*. New York: New Press, 2010.

Aukofer, Frank A. *City with a Chance: A Case History of Civil Rights Revolution*. Milwaukee, WI: Marquette University Press, 2007.

Cutler, Richard W. *Greater Milwaukee's Growing Pains, 1950–2000*. Milwaukee, WI: Milwaukee County Historical Society, 2001.

Gurda, John. *The Making of Milwaukee*. Milwaukee, WI: Milwaukee County Historical Society, 1999, 2006.

———. *One People, Many Paths: A History of Jewish Milwaukee*. Milwaukee, WI: Jewish Museum Milwaukee, 2009.

Jones, Patrick D. *The Selma of the North: Civil Rights Insurgency in Milwaukee*. Cambridge, MA: Jones Harvard University Press, 2009.

Obama, Barack. *Dreams from My Father*. New York: Three Rivers Press, 1995.

Page, Scott E. *The Difference: How the Power of Diversity Creates Better Groups, Firms and Societies*. Princeton, NJ: Princeton University, 2007.

Pager, Devah. *Marked: Race, Crime and Finding Work in an Era of Mass Incarceration*. Chicago: The University of Chicago Press, 2007.

Putman, Robert. *Bowling Alone: The Collapse and Revival of American Community*. New York: Simon and Schuster, 2000.

Rozga, Margaret. *200 Nights and One Day*. Hopkins, MN: Benu Press, 2009.

Saltman, Juliet. *A Fragile Movement: The Struggle for Neighborhood Stabilization*. New York: Greenwood Press, 1990.

Valent, Edward, and Gregory Squire. *Sherman Park, Milwaukee, Cityscape, a Journal of Policy Development and Research.* Washington, D.C.: U.S. Department of Housing and Urban Development, Office of Policy Development and Research, 1998.

INDEX

ABOUT THE AUTHOR

Paul Geenen is the author of *Milwaukee's Bronzeville: 1900–1950* by Arcadia Publishing and *Schuster's and Gimbels: Milwaukee's Beloved Department Stores* with The History Press. He moved to Sherman Park in 1976 and raised his four children there. Paul chaired the Housing Committee and was president of Sherman Park Community Association from 1979 to 1981. He is a retired entrepreneur, a grandfather of eight and a community activist. He plays tennis and racquetball and sails.